WAITING FOR CHARLIE

MERCENARY SOLDIERS, FAILED STATES, AND THE LOVE THAT MEANS MORE THAN MONEY

SUSAN ZAKIN

Markham Books, a subsidiary of Cowgirls and Pirates Media, LLC, P.O. Box 3, Valatie, NY 12184

Failed states are always somewhere else.

John Comaroff, *Theory from the South*

ONE

THE RED HILLS OF ANTANANARIVO

I went to Madagascar to understand America. But it was more than that.

I wanted to understand the Sonoran Desert, a land of heat so intense the summer air seemed to vibrate, 120,000 square miles in Arizona and the Mexican state of Sonora, a place that had become my lover, my friend, my family, my ground, a place I adopted only to realize that I was witnessing a genocide.

After my brother died in a bus collision in Nepal, I moved to the desert and watched death stuck on repeat: a house cat bloodied by a coyote, the desert tortoise that no longer appeared near my washing machine, an owl whose presence had to be hidden so people wouldn't murder it, the desert bighorn that fled the Catalina mountains. They weren't lost to predators or natural mortality. They were being driven into extinction. By us. If there was such a thing as Original Sin, I thought, this was it, Ahab minus the grandeur, humans playing God. But it was God as Destroyer, not Creator.

Of course, it was my brother who had disappeared. One

day he was in the parking lot outside a restaurant in Emeryville, California talking about his trip to Thailand and Nepal; a few weeks later, I got the call from my mother that he wasn't coming back.

I would have held him closer if I had known.

IT WAS 2001, six months before the towers fell, and our sense of ourselves, and our country, changed forever. In Madagascar, a country of red hills whose Southwest is so much like our own, I searched for an analogue for my disappearing home. For what is home without its inhabitants? Our relatives, close or distant: chimps, gorillas, orangutans, lemurs, down to sea anemones. We are all related and when one of us goes, all our lives are diminished.

In Madagascar I found remnants of life from 160 million years ago, when Madagascar split off from Africa, and 90 million years ago, when the rogue island sheared away from India to become the world's fourth-largest island. Isolation, with its disproportionate gifts of abundance and deprivation, had turned Madagascar into a Darwinian paradise. It is one of the world's great repositories of endemism, a hotbed of species that exist nowhere else. Eighty percent of the world's chameleon species can be found only in Madagascar. Lemurs, the prosimians outcompeted by monkeys in the rest of the world, survived here; that is,m until people came.

Humans, as always, the problem, sailing from Indonesia in outriggers, crossing the Mozambique Channel in dhows, and later, from Europe, plying the Atlantic in Dutch *hoekers* equipped for the slave trade. In the 1700s, pirates founded the free colony of Libertaria on Ile St. Marie, or so legend has it.

Successive waves of humanity drove fairytale creatures into extinction: the pygmy hippopotamus, the giant fossa, nine-foot-tall elephant birds. Humans brought the same trouble when they arrived in North America twelve thousand years ago. Dire wolf, short-faced bear, giant sloth, lost, all lost. But in Madagascar the blood trail is more recent.

Madagascar's lemurs and chameleons, *memento mori*, offered what I craved: Time stopped, future and past *a cette moment*, a frame for all that I had lost.

TRAVEL HAS a way of thwarting expectations. To start with, I had to work my way over. Not to complain; teaching journalism is hardly shoveling coal in the belly of a tramp steamer, but it meant getting stuck for six weeks in Antananarivo, Madagascar's capital.

There are no lemurs in Antananarivo except in the zoo. Tana, as it is familiarly known, is the second most polluted city in the world, choking with deep-fried leaded gasoline fumes from ancient Peugeots and Renaults, mixed with the rankest odors of humanity: sweat, shit, piss.

More than a million people live in the city. There is no sewage treatment plant. Everything goes into the canal. The canal drains to the river. The problem, says the official at the country's newly created environmental agency, is not the lack of a treatment plant. It is squatters living along the sewage canal who dump their trash into the canal, he cluck clucks *en français*, impeding the flow of raw sewage to the river.

The unemployment rate in Madagascar is something like forty-five percent. In the private sector, Madagascar lives off vanilla, ruby, and sapphire smuggling. In actuality, the country relies on funding from the International Monetary Fund, the World Bank and U.S. AID.

Mothers with children beg from me. Five-year olds carrying their baby sisters or brothers beg from me. Twelve-year-old girls follow me down the street saying, "Give me money."

I get used to it.

Poverty is only part of the story. On streets lined with beggars, living in worse squalor than I ever imagined, there is otherworldly transport. Most often, it is Malagasy music, an analogue for a culture too gentle to fight off conquerors, people who have not yet fully experienced the neocapitalist fervor gripping the world.

"It's an escape, the music," says a British scientist.

In front of the cobblestoned steps leading to the French colonial Hotel Colbert, a deformed man curls on the ground, his hands and feet tiny yams wrenched from the earth. Their pink bottoms bear stains like signs, maps of dark, burrowing soil.

The man plays guitar. He plucks with toeless feet like anteater's noses. He is remarkably good.

Soon I will dream of America. A certain image of the United States comes to mind, those white strips of paper that cordon off toilet seats in countless motels, proud banners that announce "Sanitized" certifying that we have left behind medieval darkness. Darkness is not buried in our memories. It has been surgically removed. But it regrows, a cancer of scattered, profligate cells. It is life, too.

Weeks after my return, the towers fall. History's gyroscope spins.

In Antananarivo, breathless from bad air, I climb the city's highest hill, looking for the Queen's Palace. I ask directions from a young couple but instead of explaining the route, they walk me to the top of the hill. Behind gates is the palace, stripped to hollow magnificent bones, half-destroyed by an arson fire in the mid-1990s, a looming commentary on history, syncretism, the ruin of the old, nothing new offered as replacement.

We run into other English speakers at a restaurant. Together all six of us hunt down a South African guy named Ray for reasons that turn out to be unimportant. Ray blasts the foreign aid that comes into the country.

"They should just leave them alone," he says.

People in the West offer the same prescription for Indian reservations. *Leave them alone*. But we cannot.

We bid each other farewell. It is almost dusk. The day has gone, my first in Madagascar.

Over the next months, this will happen to me countless times, meeting people who spend hours or days helping me as I bumble around, asking nothing in return. Delicie, the chic owner of a large business, figures out quickly that my French is inadequate. She spends an entire afternoon on the telephone helping me make appointments. We laugh at the incongruity. This thirty-one-year-old CEO, one of the country's most successful women entrepreneurs is effectively posing as my secretary.

This is what blows people's minds about Madagascar. The people are, well, nice. They're friendly. They're not in a rush. Despite the stunning disparity between my income and theirs, they don't look at me and see a dollar sign, at least most of them don't.

In short, they're like the best Americans. I wonder if the most painful consequence of the greedfest we're suffering will be the loss of America's small-town warmth.

Can time stop? Only in Shangri-La. When cult guitarists Henry Kaiser and David Lindley traveled to the island to play with Malagasy musicians, they called the CD they made "A World Out of Time." I comfort myself that it will take more than the opening of the country's first multi-national mine, which is on the boards, to change Malagasy culture. The French couldn't do it in almost a hundred years of brutal colonization.

The discovery of oil might do it. That's coming, or so I hear.

Still, it will take time.

Even the stinking crowded city of Tana has a certain charm. At dusk, the city glows paintbox colors of a Mediterranean hill town. The sun falls behind glowing hills, the city poised to enter a dream.

From somewhere outside my field of vision, I hear the sound of Malagasy music, as delicate as a small bird, as gentle as breathing. The music transforms the night, the city, the country. The world.

How can one not wish to return?

TWO
WAITING FOR CHARLIE

Behind me at the checkpoint, a ginger-haired man smokes vociferously. He's traveling light but his muscular companion is laden like a pack animal, luggage strapped across his chest like carbines. The long, hard-sided carrier he cradles in his arms suggests he's here to catch tarpon or shoot video. Record-breaking tarpon, the silver-flanked fish known for their hard fighting, do ply the Atlantic off the coast of Sierra Leone. But these travelers have earmarks of their profession: sartorial scruffiness and the sharp-eyed attentiveness of jackals.

"Reporters?" I ask.

BBC, the ginger-haired smoker says. Based in Nairobi.

"What brings you here?"

"Any excuse to come to Sierra Leone," he quips.

Yeah, right. They must be extraditing Charles Taylor. Finally.

THE ENTIRE COUNTRY was waiting for Charlie. As president of neighboring Liberia, Charles Taylor instigated a war that convulsed four countries, killed more than a quarter of a million people, mutilated an estimated 30,000, and traumatized just about everyone. In 2005, when I traveled to Sierra Leone, Taylor had been forced to resign Liberia's presidency. Indicted by a war crimes tribunal, he had fled to Nigeria, while authorities tried to extradite him But his exile could only be considered hardship by dictator standards. Living in an historic mansion on the Cross River, Taylor plotted to regain power.

Africans are so good at waiting, they forget what they are waiting for is a phrase bruited about by old Africa hands. I heard it first from a war photographer who spent a year as an investigator for Sierra Leone's Special Court, tasked with prosecuting those who bore "the greatest responsibility" for turning Sierra Leone and Liberia into poster children for failed states. Everybody was waiting for Charlie. It would be years before he showed up, and by then, would it matter?

West Africa's dirty wars of the 1990s were more than a body count, more even than an historical phenomenon of civil society starved into submission until it gave way to a gangster state. The cautionary tale needs to be witnessed by Americans, as their politicians brandish the shibboleth of independence as a mask for unleashing corruption, but the lesson of Sierra Leone goes deeper than that. When the constraints placed on people by civil society are loosed, the brutality that rises to the surface raises more existential questions, including what it means to be human. That was the question I had come to Sierra Leone to answer.

BY 2005, when I arrived in Sierra Leone, all the major figures accused of war crimes had either died or faced trial, except for Taylor. Whether it was witchcraft or the less supernatural advantages of money and power, Taylor had flouted the war crimes tribunal for two years.

In Freetown, Sierra Leone's capital, Taylor's name was on everyone's lips. His absence was like a presence. People spoke of him with such awe that it was almost as if Taylor was in charge. In a part of the world where people believe in magic, few believed a gaggle of lawyers and judges could reduce Charles Taylor to the merely human.

In the end, we discovered that Taylor was a man, after all, mortal and vulnerable. In 2006, under pressure from the administration of George W. Bush, Nigerian president Olusegun Obasanjo remanded Taylor to authorities and in 2012, Charles Taylor became the first head of state convicted by an international tribunal since the Nuremberg trials. Taylor, by then sixty-four years old, was given a fifty-year sentence. The following year, the Court of the Hague reaffirmed his sentence on appeal. He was sent to prison in Britain, where it was believed he was less likely to escape. (The fear was not unfounded; Taylor had escaped from a Massachusetts prison in his youth, an escape many believed the Central Intelligence Agency had facilitated.) In later years, Taylor's requests to be transferred to Africa were denied.

The dirty wars were finally over, or so it seemed. If Taylor's story had been written by Shakespeare or Euripedes, order would be restored amid the wreckage. But this was life, not theater.

Taylor's conviction was held up as a victory for international justice. But the victory was short-lived. In 2016, South Africa and the Gambia threatened to leave the International Criminal Court, arguing that the court unfairly targeted African leaders. Court officials argued that prosecutions had been initiated by the countries themselves but to no avail. In 2017 Burundi formally withdrew from the treaty that had established the court.

The United States was in no position to criticize, having withdrawn from the treaty soon after it established the court in 2002, along with Israel and the Sudan. To this day, the United States, fearing that its enemies outnumber its friends, refuses to subject itself to the ICC's authority.

Issues of jurisprudence aside, the most reliable sources I found in Sierra Leone insisted that prosecuting Taylor was mainly symbolic. Taylor was a symptom, not a cause. The genesis of the problem lay elsewhere.

While he was anything but innocent, making Taylor responsible for the implosion of the state in Sierra Leone was only one of a cascade of misconceptions, starting with this one: Charles Taylor was not, fundamentally, a warlord, as the Western press described him. He was not an aberration.

He was us.

CHARLES MCARTHUR GHANKAY TAYLOR grew up in Monrovia, Liberia's capital, and like many middle-class Africans, he attended college in the United States. When he was vying for the presidency, Taylor took his mother's ethnic name "Ghankay" to win adherents, but his father, a school teacher, was a Creole, which meant he was part of Liberia's elite. Descended from the freed American slaves who landed on the West African coast in the late eighteenth century, the settlers known as Creoles recreated the inequalities they had fled, dominating the country that came to be known as Liberia.

Liberia was the repository for freed slaves from the United States; Sierra Leone was where England dispatched its former slaves. While the resettlement was couched in uplifting terms, politicians in both countries were counting votes, as Israel would later do with Palestinians, recognizing that full citizenship for disenfranchised minorities could seriously upset the established order. But for supporters like William Wilberforce, one of the abolitionists popularly known as The Saints, the good intentions were genuine. The ships carrying liberated Africans from England, Nova Scotia, and Jamaica to Freetown in 1787 were bankrolled by Wilberforce and others, and Sierra Leone was given the epithet "The Province of Freedom." Both Liberia and Sierra Leone were designed as utopias that would vivify Enlightenment ideas: the separation of powers promulgated by the *philosophe* Montesquieu and the social contract prescribed by John Locke "the father of liberalism." The United States was created out of the same whole cloth, and like Liberia and Sierra Leone, the country's founders gave little thought to the inhabitants already living there.

Taylor's U.S. alma mater, Bentley University, is ranked in the top 20 of U.S. business schools. Bentley's alumni include a former governor of Massachusetts, a Radio Shack COO, a retired CEO of American Express -- and Taylor, whose CV reveals a man who reached similar heights in his chosen field: "Charles Taylor '77, Convicted war criminal; African Warlord; 22nd President of Liberia."

Warlord was the epithet the media hung on Taylor, but a Tuareg rebel chieftain of my acquaintance, a real warlord who trained in Moammar Qaddafi's training camps, scoffs at the idea. He never met Taylor there, he said, although he heard of him spending time in Tripoli with Qaddafi. "He would have gotten his silk shirt dirty!" the Tuareg laughed.

As a young man, Taylor was a familiar type, the B student who excels once he gets out into the real world. A hustler, in a word. But later events would reveal that Taylor had learned his lessons well. Shortly before Taylor's freshman year, *The New York Times Magazine* published University of Chicago economist Milton Friedman's article called "The Social Responsibility of Business is to Increase its Profits." Friedman and his neoliberal followers were reviving eighteenth-century economist David Ricardo's theory of comparative advantage; roughly speaking, the idea that each country should concentrate on the form of economic activity it does most efficiently. That theory helped propel many African countries into the world market, but there was often a price to pay. Driven by international development funders like the World Bank and the International Monetary Fund, many African farmers switched to a single crop; coffee, perhaps. When world coffee prices collapsed, or cotton, or oil, people starved. In the U.S., Ricardo's theories meant that manufacturing simply wasn't cost-effective, so corporations off-shored manufacturing jobs, breaking the power of unions and destroying a traditional ladder to the middle class for blue-collar families, immigrants, and African-Americans. Later, of course, white-collar jobs left, too, from accounting to call centers.

For less industrialized countries, globalization kicked off a new iteration of the Great Game: the bargain basement sell-off of raw materials. In the early 1990s, bankrolled by Libya's Qaddafi, Taylor gained control of Liberia's timber and rubber, including forests in the country's national parks that were supposed to be off-limits to logging. Taylor enriched himself by selling off these raw materials to companies in Europe and the U.S.

Partnering with a former TV cameraman and army veteran named Foday Sankoh, to whom he'd been introduced by Qaddafi, Taylor bankrolled Sierra Leone's rebel movement. Sierra Leone contained three percent of the world's diamonds, which Taylor knew would provide trading stock for weapons and money laundering. Over the next few years, as Sankoh's rebels terrorized Sierra Leone and neighboring Cote D'Ivoire and Guinea erupted into violence, the conventional wisdom has it that Taylor had singlehandedly destabilized four West African countries.

Many contemporary Africa scholars characterize his accomplishments differently: Taylor developed an alternative social structure based purely on power, money, and fear. You could say that Taylor's West Africa in the 1990s is what happens when capitalism is free of any restraint. Reporters called Liberia "Charles Taylor, Inc."

What does pure libertarianism look like? It looks like the footless amputee hovering grimly at the Freetown airport. If any one person could be considered responsible for the deaths of hundreds of thousands of people, the amputations of arms and legs, the rapes and tortures, the defilement of thousands of children, most people would say it is Taylor. What is the proper response to a holocaust? In the 1940s, it was a court in Nuremberg, Germany. In 2005, the international community was trying the same remedy.

But what if they had the wrong man?

JET-LAGGED from twenty hours of travel, I stare numbly at the motionless baggage carousel. When it finally creaked into action, I watched every form of luggage imaginable, from plaids to Samsonite, not to mention cardboard boxes. But my bag did not appear. The reporters smirked as they trotted off with their suitcases. Across the carousel a woman erupted into ear-splitting screams. I couldn't see much through the crowd, but it sounded as through the police were trying, fruitlessly, to calm her.

Spotting my suitcase, I quickly shouldered my way past two burly men to grab it. Neither offered to lift my bag from the carousel. Fair enough, I thought. Women can't expect that kind of treatment anymore. But they didn't even get out of my way. As I rolled my bag toward customs, the police were still trying to calm the woman. Her screams had dropped in decibel level but she sounded inconsolable.

A tout led me to a kiosk to buy tickets for the helicopter that would ferry me to Freetown. Freetown's airport was built at the tip of a marshy peninsula impassable by road. The location made no sense until it was explained to me that the land was purchased with *boku* aid money from one of the president's cronies. I'd gotten instructions for making it to the city: the ferry was cheaper but it had a tendency to sink and the hydrofoil was safer but often out for repairs. I was bone-tired so I went for the most expensive option, a helicopter.

At the ticket window, I tried not to stare at the man on crutches. He had only one foot, the other presumably amputated in the war. I should have expected it. Sierra Leone is known for its amputees the way a red-garbed Beefeater symbolizes Jolly Olde England. Only it was two a.m. and in these airports at night – why is it one always arrives at night? – there is always a feeling of a dream.

A uniformed man motioned us out to the tarmac. The helicopter's op art paint job managed a nod to Richard Branson's Virgin hipster jets. Nice try, I thought, but nothing could make the Soviet Mi-8 look like anything but what it is: a lumbering beast designed to withstand bullets. The Mi-8 is the workhorse of military helicopters, and, man, was it loud. Rotor noise filled the airspace like onomatopoeia. The Atlantic breeze disappeared into the vortex, the runway lights dulled, even the choking humidity seemed to shatter against the blades. There was only the roar, a horrific noise borne on the rotors' gale, sweeping us all in its wake.

BEFORE THE WAR, the Cape Sierra was the swankest hotel in Sierra Leone. The architecture has that unmistakable Brutalist Jetsons look, lots of concrete and weird curves. Built in the 1970s in preparation for a meeting of the Organization of Africa States by the country's president Siaka Stevens, a former trade unionist who had seized power in 1968, the hotel lobby, glimpsed through my bleary middle-of-the night eyes, looked like Hefner's mansion in old copies of *Playboy*.

In daylight, the Cape Sierra was about the same, overcalled but cracked with age and disrepair and humidity: the walls, the floors, the furniture, all preserved under a sheen of yellowing sweat. Running water was iffy, but the air conditioners worked and I had a window to the Atlantic: grey-blue water, waves white with foam, and in the distance, green turrets of mountains clasping the shore. Through the thick trees, Africans were kicking a soccer ball along the shoreline.

Sierra Leone was no longer a colony when the Cape Sierra was built, but the hotel has an unmistakably colonial air. Every few hours the staff rakes up the white magnolia petals that have fallen like dissolving ermine on the lawn. The swimming pool is enormous and deeply blue. Blonde British women lie on plastic chaises. It's unwise to take your wallet to the beach, and so, unless you are accompanied, it is not worth the trouble to go. Better to swim in the pool. "The man here is very good. No need to worry," they assure me. The *thwock* of tennis balls is heard in the distance.

The hotel is also quite large, and this is another reason a delegation from the U.S. is coming here. A professor named Joe Opala has organized a trip whose centerpiece is a Thomalind Martin Polite, a thirty-four-year-old speech pathologist from Charleston. Thomalind is the seventh-generation descendant of a child kidnapped into slavery in 1756. African-American homecomings have become a fixture of the African tourism business, but generally they are confined to countries that have been war-free and provide amenities for tourists, places like Ghana and Senegal, countries where the U.N. headquarters is not a blackened hulk and the locals possess the usual number of limbs. African-American homecomings can be seen as healing pilgrimages, sentimental delusions, or both. In certain parts of Africa, the locals call black American tourists "whites" because they have money. It is only Americans who define a person exclusively by the color of their skin.

Am I on a pilgrimage? In a way. I have personal reasons for being here, research for a novel I'm writing. Later, as I immersed myself in books about the so-called "dirty wars," I became fixated on a more existential question. "How can people be so cruel?" kept recurring to me, a line I'd heard it as a kid in a song from the hippie Broadway musical Hair. Maybe it was something I needed to answer about my own life. As writers often do, I found that a degree of separation made it easier to extract meaning. To fund my trip, I had wangled an assignment to churn out a tacky inspirational piece for a Sunday supplement on Thomalind's journey to her ancestor's home, so there I was, interview the Scheherazade whose account of his time in Sierra Leone had gotten me started on the whole thing: Joe Opala.

OPALA and I had agreed to meet in the hotel lounge, a sunken living room affair, and he was late. As I sat nursing a Coke, one of the women at the bar caught my eye. She smiled at me and I smiled back. Then she got up from her barstool and walked to where I was sitting at one of the low tables.

"Hi," she said, holding out her hand. She had long braids and large gaps between her teeth.

"Hi," I said, shaking her hand.

"I'm Nyonontee," she said.

I told her my name.

"How are you?" she asked.

"Fine," I said. "And you?"

"Oh, fine, fine. I saw you over there. You are very pretty."

"Well, thanks," I said.

"Are you alone?" she asked.

"I'm waiting for someone."

"He is not here?"

"He's late."

"We can be friends?" she asked.

"Well, we can talk a bit," I said. I hesitated, but good manners won out. "Why don't you sit down?"

"Thank you."

"Are you from Freetown?" I asked.

"Oh, I come from Liberia. I come to Freetown when I am fifteen years old."

"That's pretty young."

"My family had hard times," she said. "These men give me a chance to come to Freetown. To the beach." She shrugged.

Joe arrived. Nyonontee jumped up as if stung with a hot iron.

"Joe?"

We shook hands.

"This is Nyonontee."

They shook hands.

"I don't want to interrupt," Joe said.

"No, no," said Nyonontee, backing away.

"No, no, no," I said, not quite knowing why I was saying it, too. I didn't want Nyonontee to feel badly, I suppose.

"I'll see you sometime?" she said to me in parting. "We'll be friends?"

"Sure," I told her. "Maybe I'll see you in the bar."

Nyonontee smiled uncertainly.

"Was she hitting on you?" Joe asked once she was out of earshot.

"No, of course not," I said, blinking. *I'm a woman. Why would she be hitting on me?*

I inadvertently glanced over at Nyonontee. Flashing a big, gap-toothed smile, she waved.

Finding my way around this country suddenly seemed a tad more challenging.

JOE HAD BEEN a Peace Corps volunteer in the Sixties. After his stint in Sierra Leone, he went to graduate school, completing his coursework but never finishing his dissertation. Instead, he headed back to Sierra Leone, where he taught at Fourah Bay College, West Africa's first Western-style university, founded in 1827. Over the next seventeen years, he watched the disintegration of his adopted country. By the mid-1990s, his political activities made it dangerous for him to stay. He waited until the very last minute before boarding the last helicopter evacuating people from the roof of the Mammy Yoko Hotel.

Joe was called into the State Department the Africa staff, and he seemed to be in a constant state of irritation over the apparent inability of Americans to understand Sierra Leone. For the next hour, he gave me a crash course in the country's recent. It was a story with an arc that would become familiar to me as I learned more about Africa, the golden period immediately following independence followed by a downward trajectory with the elements of a Shakespearean tragedy.

The country's first prime minister after independence was Sir Milton Augustus Streibi Margai, a friend of the British, and the first man from the interior to earn a medical degree. Margai promoted health care and literacy for women. He was a modest fellow, by all accounts. Even after he became president, he drove his own car and haggled over the price of fish with market women.

After Sir Milton's death in 1964, his half-brother Albert Margai became prime minister. Albert was not only less intelligent than his brother, he was also corrupt. Albert Margai's administration set the stage for his successor, the brilliant former trade unionist Siaka Stevens, who consolidated power by changing the constitution, packing the courts, and trumping up charges against his enemies. A large man with a penchant for Savile Row suits and a thyroidic glare only partially masked by false bonhomie, he made Sierra Leone his personal fiefdom, while the people of the diamond-rich country slid into penury.

As Joe told it, Stevens retired in 1985, just ahead of a coup. His vice president, a nonentity named Joseph Momoh, inherited the country's problems. To hear Joe tell it, Momoh's high point was describing Stevens as "a seventeen-year plague of locusts" in his inaugural speech. Other than that, it was corruption as usual.

In 1992, young officers from The Tigers, Sierra Leone's version of Special Forces, staged a coup d'etat. The Boys, as many called them, lost control of the provinces fairly quickly, but they managed to hold power in Freetown for the next four years. The countryside devolved into chaos: burning, looting, murder, drugged child soldiers, and, of course, the amputations that hold an adolescent fascination for the media.

Here's the interesting part. The Boys remained popular, long after they lost control of the country. They kept the streets of Freetown clean, sending soldiers out to hold neighborhood cleanups at gunpoint. After I had picked my way around piles of stinking garbage in Freetown for a few weeks, I began to understand why this endeared The Boys to regular citizens in Freetown. There was almost a familial feeling in Sierra Leone, and The Boys were like everyone's sons or younger brothers. They epitomized hope, as children do.

In 1996, under pressure from pro-democracy activists and the international community, Julius Maada Bio, who had been one of the young coup leaders, resigned the presidency. He was only twenty-seven. In an election deemed fair, a former United Nations official named Tejan Kabbeh won the presidency. The country devolved into a warlord state after a coup in 1999, but a few months later Kabbeh was reinstated. Along with Kabbeh, "the permanent government" returned, corrupt ministers and their clients: diamond traders, timber companies, you name it.

"All the things that happened here," I paused, with something, I hoped, approaching delicacy – "they say it's worse than Kosovo..."

"You mean ten thousand mutilations?" Joe asked.

"Well, right. Is there something in the culture...."

"Would you ask that about Iraq?" Joe bellowed. "A lot of people are losing their hands there, too. It's just different because they're pushing a button from 10,000 feet in the air. You reporters!"

Joe was parroting the party line among the human rights crowd. *U.S. bombs in Iraq are blowing off people's extremities, too, you know.* But surely it must feel different to look someone in the eye when you drop a *panga* on their arm versus dropping a bomb through cloud cover. From thirty thousand feet, your accuser is your own imagination. Later, in fact, I would read a study indicating that the unseen victim creates more lasting trauma in the soldier who kills. Besides, who on earth came up with the horrible idea of cutting off people's hands and feet? Apart from the barnyard brutality, the victims would be unable to earn a living for the rest of their lives. At least the physical torture in Guantanamo ended when someone was released. These victims were consigned to a lifetime of torture.

"This is a *political* process," Joe said. "Siaka Stevens systematically dismantled civil society in Sierra Leone. It has nothing to do with being *primitive*."

Hoping to atone for my blunder, I merely nodded. What did any of this have to do with Charles Taylor? Americans and Europeans, including court officials, continued to believe that all roads led to bringing Taylor to justice. Could one man's punishment rebuild a country?

I asked Joe what he thought of the attempt to extradite Taylor. Nothing, he replied. The war crimes court would do no good unless it prosecuted the corrupt "permanent government" of Sierra Leone. But that was not the court's brief.

SUSAN SONTAG, in *Regarding the Pain of Others*, wrote of "the professional, specialized tourists known as journalists." Apart from the Roots people, the only outsiders who come to Sierra Leone are Sontag's specialized tourists: reporters, U.N. personnel, aid workers, professors. Perhaps Sierra Leone could be marketed: The Failed State Tour, Summer 2005! Buy your black t-shirts here.

On the second day of the trip, I played hooky from the *Roots* journey to attend the war crimes tribunal. The Special Court is a strikingly modern building with a split roof that rises like the wings of an enormous bird of prey. The court was rotating trials among the three factions in the civil war. When I was there, the court was prosecuting the leaders of the Civil Defense Force. This was the consortium of village-based militias headed by the Sandhurst-educated Sam Hinga Norman. When the Sierra Leone army had become untrustworthy because of its alliance with the rebels, then-president Ahmed Tejan Kabbah consolidated the village militias, designating them as the government's security force.

The Kamajors, fighters from the Mende tribe in the eastern part of the country, dominated the civil defense forces. Their top three leaders are currently on trial. Not everyone is happy about this. Many people in Sierra Leone see the Kamajors as heroes. If they committed atrocities, the attitude is, well, everyone was doing it and at least it was for a good cause.

This is a political problem for the court, but there isn't much to be done about it. David Crane, the former Special Forces paratrooper and U.S. Department of Defense investigator who heads the Special Court, says it's simply too bad. Nobody is above the law.

Except, perhaps, Taylor. But Crane refuses to admit the possibility that Taylor will elude prosecution and remain at large, living large, in his mansion in Nigeria.

I WASN'T PLAYING hooky alone. Jim Campbell, the Brown professor, had once been a reporter, and he had asked to come along. As we sat on the benches watching the court proceedings, we found ourselves chatting with a young reporter named Joseph who had been covering the trial for more than a year.

"Do you remember the coup?" the lawyer asked.

"Which one?" I whispered to Joseph. He laughed quietly, behind his hand.

We watched as a twenty-five-year-old woman testified, or more accurately, we listened. To protect her identity, her back was turned to the gallery. For added protection, she sat inside a trifold screen.

The woman was from Kenema, one of the cities that kept falling; falling to the rebels, falling to the army, and finally, falling to the Kamajors, the traditional fighters who believed bullets bounced off their bodies, the way the Ghost Dancers in the American West believed they could withstand the bullets of the American cavalry.

The Kamajors weren't such good guys, it seems. They tied up her brother, dropped a tire around his neck, and lit it on fire.

He was crying out our mother's name.

"But the Kamajors weren't as bad as the rebels, right?" I whispered to Joseph.

"They killed everyone," Joseph whispered back.

"They'd say, 'Bring me ten heads.' The soldiers would go and kill people. They were gods."

AFTER I LEFT SIERRA LEONE, I tried to find answers to the question I had asked Joe Opala. In addition to chopping off people's hands and feet, there were reports of cannibalism among soldiers during the war, particularly the Kamajors. When I asked anthropologist Rosalind Shaw about this, she was equally reluctant to make a connection between traditional religious practices and wartime atrocities. When I called her at Stanford University, Shaw even claimed that she didn't know whether cannibalism existed before the war. In fact, she suggested, Europeans might be the true cannibals.

"Cannibalism has been a metaphor in Sierra Leone ever since the slave trade so it's impossible to know when you hear a report of cannibalism," she said. "In Sierra Leone, as in many parts of west Africa, white people were thought of as cannibals. Why were taking all these shiploads of black people off? Rumors flew that they were being carried off to be butchered and eaten. As a metaphor for the slave trade it's not too far off, they were being consumed, their bodies were consumed. We just can't take reports of cannibalism literally."

When I repeated her theory to a Sierra Leonean political activist about this, he laughed, and then he regaled me with stories of cannibalism that he remembered from his youth. Like Americans fascinated by tales of African cannibals, Sierra Leoneans blamed the Liberians. "Don't wander at night," the man's mother used to tell him. "The Liberians will get you!"

Cannibalism clearly existed in West Africa, just as it

did in many places in the world, including the American southwest, at various times in human history. Australian anthropologist Laurence R. Goldman suggests that cannibalism exists as "an entrenched metaphor of cultural xenophobia," so in a certain way, the way people view cannibalism is as revealing as the practice itself.

To Westerners, cannibalism is the unthinkable act that divides the "civilized" world's discontents from the externalized demons of the bush. In his 1999 book, *Mask of Anarchy*, a study of Liberia's civil war, Stephen Ellis documents the history of flesh-eating and human sacrifice, and suggests that the practice has persisted, modernized to reflect the realities of neoliberal capitalism.

It starts with the secret societies endemic to West African society. For as long as anyone can remember, boys in Liberia, Sierra Leone, and Guinea have been initiated into manhood in Poro, a secret society, while girls were initiated into a secret society called Sande. George Way Harley, an American missionary who lived for thirty-four years in Liberia and studied Poro, said that the Poro may be thought of as "an attempt to reduce the all pervading spirit world" to something that man can interpret, where "men became spirits, and took on godhead."

In their Poro initiation, boys go to a special village in the forest where they are taught the virtues of discipline, courage, and obedience, "rather like an old-fashioned English public school," Ellis wrote. Initiates who failed weren't flogged or buggered, though. They're killed and their hearts are eaten, or their livers.

When the others return to their homes, they are received as newcomers, as if they had been reborn. Their old selves died in the forest; eaten by the Bush Devil. The boys who didn't make it through the initiation? The *desparecidos*? Blame it on the Bush Devil.

"Poro business is eating business," the saying goes.

In Sierra Leone and Liberia, as in many parts of Africa, the word *eat* is almost like the word *love* in America, or, even more accurately, *grok* in the old sci-fi novel *Stranger in a Strange Land*; it has many meanings, depending on the context. Eating is the foundation, at least in a symbolic sense, for power relations and for the acquisition of wealth, often by any means necessary.

"The bosses, they eat the money and don't pay them," a soldier told me, explaining corruption in the Sierra Leone Army.

When war broke out in Sierra Leone, it had been little more than a century since the British outlawed the practice of eating human flesh, so it's not surprising that the language still contained clues to the importance of human sacrifice. Cannibalism didn't end with prohibition, of course. The secret societies already had a tradition of secrecy, so the British ban only pushed them further into the forest depths. The most secret of all was the Human Leopard Society.

The Human Leopard Society was for elite older men, a West African version of the Rotary Club. Ellis writes about the difficulty of discerning the exact nature of the leopard societies before colonialism. One of the most earliest accounts is from a British colonial commission of inquiry in Sierra Leone, which found Human Leopard Societies dating back to the 1850s. The commission reported that "men of mature age, past their prime met in secret conclave and regularly killed human victims in a form of sacrifice". They ate the flesh of their victims "with a view to increasing their virile powers." They used fat from their victims' bodies to feed a cult object called the Borfima, which was described as a lump of black wax wrapped with bits of cloth and leopard skin. When the wax cracked, the Borfima must be fed, according to another colonial account.

What does this have to do with West Africa now, a place where teenagers are addicted to Facebook and rap music blares from street side speakers? Culture doesn't disappear overnight, or even in several generations. Blaine Harden, one of the clearest-thinking journalists to cover Africa, has written: "Europeans overwhelmed the continent in the last quarter of the nineteenth century, looking for loot. They carved it up into weirdly shaped money-making colonies, many of them landlocked, all of them administered from the top down. The colonies bore little or no relation to existing geographical or tribal boundaries. Total conquest took all of about twenty-five years. Then, after sixty years or so – the shortest introduction to so-called civilization that any so-called primitive people have ever had – the Europeans turned their authoritarian creation over to the Africans."

Human sacrifice and cannibalism never completely disappeared in Sierra Leone and Liberia. In the 1930s, the writer Graham Greene set out to determine the veracity of the old stories. In *Journey Without Maps*, Greene writes of a trip in the Nimba range in Liberia, where the Mano people lived: "Laminah and Amedoo knew all about it. Laminah said to me one day, 'these people bad, they chop men', and they were happy to leave the Manos behind."

That was as far as Greene got, and who can blame him? In his book *Mask of Anarchy*, Steven Ellis quotes more detailed eyewitness accounts from the same time period, spanning the 1920s to the 1940s. One report comes from a German doctor who, performing an autopsy on the victim of a supposed leopard attack, arrived at the conclusion the wounds were caused by humans who had "neatly excised the liver from the body." Members of the Human Leopard Society used a bladed knife that left marks on their victims' bodies mimicking the depredations of a leopard, Ellis writes.

The phenomenon of men masquerading as leopards, or crocodiles, snakes, and baboons in similar secret societies, was related to the importance of masks in West African forest religions. When someone wears a mask, he feels he has become another being. Masks allow the use of power in stateless societies like Sierra Leone and Liberia, according to Ellis. This explains why so many of the soldiers in the conflicts of the 1990s wore women's wigs and face paint. Once the mask is removed, at least some soldiers return to their former lives with a minimum of fuss. In Sierra Leone, people say that the problems faced by at least some former child soldiers are exaggerated. In Bo, a city in eastern Sierra Leone, former child soldiers are running the city's largest taxi service. It's been very successful, although it's hard to avoid joking that nobody argues about the fares.

I studied with a poet who had us read *Antigone* and *The Odyssey*. She talked about metonymy, defined as "the substitution of the name of an attribute or adjunct for that of the thing meant, for example *suit* for *business executive*, or *the track* for *horse racing*."

What she meant by the term was something more profound. In early human societies - ancient Greece was the one she talked about - the thing itself carried meaning. This made me understand the sculptural quality of poetry and why it is the highest art form.

Over time, the balance between metaphor and metonymy may shift back and forth. Bishop Arthur Kulah, a missionary in Liberia, wrote about the son of a chief who had been initiated into Poro as a ten-year-old boy in the 1940s. The boy went on to earn a PhD. in political science in the U.S. After his return, he was elected to the Liberian senate. The elders in his district told him he must make sacrifice to purify him for the job ahead. This was either in the 1960s or 1970s. The bishop never answered the question of whether this particular senator ate human flesh, but there's no question that, even this late in the game, that cannibalism was a career move, and so it remained. A notorious videotape shows Liberian coup leader Prince Johnson ordering his thugs to kill President Samuel K. Doe as Doe whines and begs for mercy, and one version of it shows Johnson eating Doe's ear. This was September 9, 1990.

By that time, human sacrifice in Sierra Leone and Liberia had become, in Ellis' words, "subject to market principles." Members of the Human Leopard Society were less likely to sacrifice their family members, even thought this was considered the most effective form of sacrifice. (Abraham and Isaac, anyone?) Instead, they paid "heartmen" for victims. In 1995, a newspaper reporter wrote that heartmen had become "a nationwide plague until the war when it became unnecessary for one to even hide to kill for killing was the tool of the trade."

Power was taken as a sign that a person has been privileged by the spirit world. When he finally ascended to the presidency after his years in the wilderness becoming unimaginably rich as the head of a shadow government, they say Charles Taylor drank blood out of a skull.

CHARLES TAYLOR MUST HAVE BEEN a nondescript student at Bentley College, since nobody seems to remember him. But his gifts became apparent soon after graduation, when he led a 1979 demonstration protesting the policies of Liberian president William Tolbert in New York. As students rallied outside the Liberian mission to the United Nations, Tolbert challenged Taylor to a debate. Taylor accepted, and by press accounts, outshined the president. But Taylor went too far, declared he would take over the Liberian mission and he was arrested.

Instead of pressing charges, Tolbert, as the story goes, was so impressed with the young man that he offered him a job. Shortly after Taylor's return, Tolbert was deposed in a coup led by an army sergeant named Samuel K. Doe. In contrast to Tolbert and Taylor, Doe was neither educated nor Creole. The ascension of a native from the interior to the presidency signaled an epochal shift for a country that had never broken its ties to the United States. Firestone Tire and Rubber Company had been operating the largest rubber plantation in the world in Liberia since 1926, and the country was a staging ground for both operations and intelligence for the U.S. military. America's notion of itself as "land of the free" precluded the legal establishment of a colony, but Liberia was often called "a colony in all but name" of the United States.

For Taylor, Doe's coup turned out to be a business opportunity. Doe appointed him head of the country's General Services Agency, a perfect opportunity for graft. Taylor was forced to flee Liberia in 1983, accused of embezzling $900,000 to an account at Citibank. He made his way back to the U.S., where he was taken into custody while Doe's government attempted to bring him back to Liberia to face trial.

In 1985, Charles Taylor began his transformation from callow college student to Leopard Man. Taylor was being held awaiting extradition in a Plymouth, Massachusetts jail. The story goes that Taylor and three common criminals tied sheets together, sawed through the bars of their cell, and rapeled to the ground.

As is so often the case with West Africa's political history, rumors are more plausible than the few bare facts one can assemble. Taylor was suspected to have been one of the many international students subsidized by CIA funds through their college careers with the *quid pro quo* that they would make themselves available after they returned to their home countries. At the time of Taylor's escape, the Reagan administration was growing disenchanted with Doe. The unschooled president had initially fulfilled Liberia's duties as a client state of the U.S. without complaint, but now he was demanding more foreign aid and, alarmingly, negotiating with Russia.

If the CIA considered Taylor a promising young man — educated in the U.S., after all, practically one of ours — it's not unreasonable to believe the story that Taylor pulled off his Jimmy Cagney jailbreak with CIA connivance. The official story of his escape was such a cliché that it lends credence to the theory that the U.S. saw him as a potential successor to the crude Doe.

In 2009, Taylor himself testified at the Special Court for Sierra Leone in The Hague, that U.S. agents not only helped him escape, but provided the car that took him to New York, where he boarded a flight to Mexico on his own passport. According to Taylor, the U.S. had provided arms for a planned coup that failed.

CIA sources dismissed his testimony as "completely absurd." But the Defense Intelligence Agency, the Pentagon's spy arm, later disclosed in documents released under the Freedom of Information Act to the Boston Globe that its agents, and those of the CIA, did work with Taylor from the early 1980s on. The Globe later walked back the story, saying only that the agency had confirmed that it possessed records relating to Taylor and to his relationship, if any, with American intelligence going back to 1982 and that the agency, however, refused to release the documents.

Whatever his relationship ("if any") with the Americans, after the coup's failure Taylor must have considered himself a free agent - or a double agent. He headed to one of Muammar Qaddafi's training camps in Libya, the Ivy League for pan-African insurgents. A minor detail, perhaps, but a friend of mine debunked the widely reported story that the young Taylor trained as a guerrilla fighter. This man, a Tuareg prince from Niger who fought in that country's insurgencies in the 1990s, trained as a guerrilla in two of the camps, but he never heard of Taylor going through the military training. He says that he met Taylor with Foday Sankoh, a former TV cameraman for the Sierra Leone Army, who would become the leader of Sierra Leone's bloodthirsty rebel army, in Tripoli. Taylor was cutting a deal with Qaddafi, said the Tuareg, to support his military ad political ambitions. "He was never in the desert," my friend scoffed. "He would have gotten his silk shirt dirty."

A photo of Taylor from that period shows him clad in camouflage and cradling an AK-47, but there is a whiff of photo op about the image. If so, the media manipulation was well-conceived: by the 1990s, Liberia was devolving into a warlord state and a soldier named Prince Johnson commanded Liberia's Special Forces, called the Black Scorpions, while Taylor headed his own guerrilla army. Despite repeated attempts, Taylor couldn't quite manage to capture the capital city of Monrovia and many in Liberia shared the Tuareg's assessment of Taylor as slick and sophisticated, but perhaps not quite manly enough. When Johnson captured a former vice-president of the republic, he told him, "you are the first bookman I have arrested. Charles Taylor has all the book people. I am a fighter." Johnson added: "I want you to help me put some ideas together on the economic and political side of this thing."

While his marksmanship might have been in question, Taylor didn't need help with "the economic and political side." Consolidating power in the provinces, he gained control of Liberia's diamonds, gold, timber, rubber, and iron ore. In 1991-92 alone, Taylor's "Greater Liberia" produced more than 10,000 cubic feet of timber, which it exported to France, Germany, the United Kingdom, Italy, the Netherlands, Spain, Greece, Portugal, and Turkey. Liberia became France's third-largest supplier of wood.

The U.S. ambassador to Liberia estimated that Taylor was making "upwards of $75 million" a year from taxes levied on the selloff of Liberia's natural resources, including those in national parks. Ministers in Monrovia guessed it was more like $100 million. That didn't include income from marijuana grown in northern Liberia and exported in container ships. Business school was finally paying off.

While Taylor built his empire, the "legitimate" government in Monrovia was pulling in little more than a tenth of this amount, mostly from licensing ships; Liberia is the equivalent of Delaware, an offshore rubber stamp for ocean-going rogues. Governments and multinationals cut deals with Taylor, not Johnson, and by most accounts, he was a tough negotiator.

Anthropologist Svend E. Holsoe of the University of Delaware explained to Stephen Ellis that Taylor was merely following tradition. "One of the features of such 'stateless' societies was that, in the general absence of any highly institutionalized form of civic government other than the religious societies, there was considerable scope for political entrepreneurs, usually young men successful in war, to rise from obscurity to positions of influence through force of personality and the distribution of largess gained in trade or war," wrote Ellis.

Holsoe traced Taylor's path to power to an earlier wave of globalization in the late 1700s and early 1800s: "These individuals used an alternative base for achieving their positions, usually a combination of special access to economic resources outside the traditional society – most often European trade goods – and great astuteness in understanding the local political structure and manipulating it to their own purposes."

Charles Taylor may have been following tradition — and a scaleable business plan — but he was doing it with the help of drugged child soldiers fighting a civil war that eventually killed an estimated 50,000 Liberians and drove about a quarter of the population from their homes. In 1997, when Charles Taylor was elected president of Liberia, he didn't even have to rig the election. Seventy-five percent of Liberians voted for Taylor and the election was approved by the European Union and Jimmy Carter. (On election night in July 1997, Taylor reportedly told Carter that he wanted to be "a Mandela.")

What could they do? Taylor had won fair and square - sort of. His men delivered rice to bribe Liberians to vote for him, but fear played a role, too. Many Liberians said they felt the choice was between Taylor or war. "You killed my ma, you killed my pa, I vote for you," was a popular song at rallies.

Within two years, the Taylor regime's brutality and greed had become too much for Liberians. While the international community imposed economic and military sanctions, Liberian refugees formed a rebel army. It took until 2003 for Nigerian soldiers to frog march Taylor out of office by Nigerian soldiers with the support of the international community. Unwilling to countenance defeat, Taylor called it "a cooling off period." "God willing," he said, "I'll be back."

Dealing with Taylor was a sticky wicket. Presidents of neighboring countries were understandably reluctant to subject themselves to international justice, whether in the form of court proceedings or military action initiated by multinational organizations.

Nigeria was the region's anchor, a large, powerful country with massive oil wealth. Nigerian president Olusegun Obasanjo took it upon himself to offer asylum to Taylor. Obasanjo himself was no stranger to charges of human rights abuses. In the 1970s, Obasanjo's soldiers burned singer Fela Kuti's house and brutalized Kuti and his family, including his mother, who died of injuries suffered in the raid. Neither was he naive about Taylor's character. He offered Taylor refuge, but only on the condition that Taylor stayed out of politics. Adamant about the principle of national sovereignty, ostensibly to counter the continued meddling of the West, but also to protect himself, Obasanjo declared that Taylor could only be handed over to an elected Liberian government.

With elections scheduled, Taylor knew the clock was ticking. Court documents provide evidence that Taylor slipped away for secret meetings in Burkina Faso with Francis Galawolo, who announced shortly afterwards that he would be campaigning for the presidency of Liberia. While under Nigeria's protection, Taylor also allegedly received money from an Al-Qaeda operative named

Mohamed Mustafa Fahil, part of an ongoing money-laundering relationship involving diamonds that was documented by *Washington Post* reporter Douglas Farah. That money allegedly went to fund Galawolo's presidential bid. Special court officials would later charge that Taylor also violated the terms of his asylum by backing an assassination attempt against Lansana Conte, the president of Guinea. Yet Obasanjo refused to let the Special Court extradite Taylor.

As the stalemate over Taylor continued, critics questioned how hard the Bush administration was trying to get him extradited. Many felt the administration was reluctant to expose the U.S. role in Liberia, including its earlier associations with Taylor.

Truth was elusive as Taylor himself.

THE MAN CHASING Taylor is what you would get if you crossed Abraham Lincoln with the Uber-WASP actor William Hurt, adding just a dash of Savonarola. Tall, blond, hollow-cheeked and rangy, he calls himself "a product of the Sixties" but one assumes he is referring to Watergate's lessons about ethics and corruption, not dropping acid at Woodstock. Before heading the Special Court for Sierra Leone, he was director of the Office of Intelligence Review, heading the government's watchdog agency for intelligence services and assistant general counsel of the Defense Intelligence Agency. After leaving Sierra Leone for a teaching post at Syracuse University, he would start Impunity Watch, an online publication that tracks human rights violations in real time, and his students set up the Syria Accountability Project, analyzing open source materials to support the prosecution of President Bashar al-Assad and his subordinates, as well as members of the Syrian opposition suspected of war crimes.

What clicked for me when I interviewed Crane was that he had been Special Forces paratrooper. When he was chosen to set up the Special Court, his Vietnam experience was very much on his mind. At that time, in the early 2000s, the cost of international justice had gone through the roof, and there was a general feeling that the results were not sufficiently impressive. War crimes tribunals in Yugoslavia and Rwanda were costing millions of dollars and had been trundling along for a decade with no end in sight.

Crane decided to prosecute only those deemed "most responsible" for the atrocities in Sierra Leone. Making the economic case for international justice was not the only concern. Crane was also influenced by the U.S. response to a massacre of Vietnamese civilians in a village called My Lai. A low-ranking officer named William Calley was convicted while his superiors who had given the orders went free, and My Lai became a synonym for a loss of faith in America.

Crane was determined to restore that same faith in Sierra Leone. The special court would be located in Freetown, both to save money, and the hope was, to show the public that the country's justice system, which had devolved into kangaroo courts when Siaka Stevens was president, was functioning in a fair and impartial manner.

In addition to his legal credentials, Crane has a master's degree in West African history. He has his own ideas about what caused the brutality in Sierra Leone and bristles at the relativism in vogue among anthropologists like Opala and Shaw. Anthropologists, Crane points out, tend to be a self-righteous, politically correct bunch. When asked to explain how such widespread and bizarre atrocities took place in

Sierra Leone, Crane answers, channeling John Locke, that it all comes down to the social compact.

"It's a perfect example of how the rule of law tempers the basic instincts of human beings," Crane said. "There was no rule of law in West Africa. There never was. The fact that there was no rule of law is one of the reasons these individuals could do these things. You should have seen the looks in their eyes when they were being arrested. They never thought this would happen. Most of them think they will walk away from this. They have such contempt for the law. They've used the law as a tool.

"I have literally cradled these people (the victims) in my arms," he said. "I have seen the bodies. I have seen the mass graves. I have seen the living dead, the people missing breasts, lips, ears, genitalia. A woman in Makeni; literally her face was missing. She was cradling her baby. And she was saying, 'They did this to me. Seek justice.'"

One of the questions raised by the dirty wars of the 1990s is whether Western-style justice is appropriate or justified in a different cultural context. African leaders have used these culture and sovereignty arguments to their advantage. One is Kenyan President Uhuru Kenyatta, who had been accused of crimes against humanity related to election violence in 2007. After witnesses either recanted or disappeared, the ICC was forced to drop its case against Kenyatta and his vice president, William Ruto. To quell criticism, Kenyatta set up an independent war crimes tribunal in Kenya - one that is totally controlled by his own administration. Like Taylor and many of the government ministers I met in Sierra Leone, Uhuru Kenyatta was educated in America, at Amherst College in Massachusetts.

Crane's stance is that leaders like Taylor and Kenyatta can't have it both ways. "Ordinary foot soldiers are better-served by traditional rituals of reconciliation," he said. "But if a country's leaders wish to participate in the international community - accept foreign aid, vote in the United Nations - they must observe the basic tenets of international law."

But as Crane and the court's investigators prepared their cases, their attempt to make examples of the war's ruthless leaders started to crumble. Foday Sankoh, who headed the rebel forces responsible for the majority of war crimes, died in prison before his trial ended. Sam Hinga Norman, the Kamajor leader, appeared increasingly enfeebled. He remained feisty enough to challenge the court's authority, insisting that as a chief he was not subject to their authority, but died while undergoing medical treatment in Senegal before the court could rule.

The only way the court would be declare success was if Charles Taylor could be brought to trial. Nobody on the street believed it would happen. Taylor was invulnerable. A shape-shifter. *He killed my pa, he killed my ma.*

Doggedly, Crane insisted that Taylor would be extradited to Sierra Leone. How could it be otherwise?

"Charles Taylor is individually, criminally responsible for the murder, rape, and mutilation of 1.2 million human beings," said Crane.

When I arrived, Crane had been saying this for more than a year.

ONE OF THE peculiarities of Sierra Leone's decade-long civil war was that, in some places, it functioned as a highly ironic form of environmentalism. Tiwai Island, in eastern Sierra Leone, is one of the top five places in the world for primate diversity. Rare species like the olive colobus monkey flourished on the island during the war because humans were too busy shooting each other to harvest bush meat for market. At Joe Opala's suggestion, I planned a visit there, and persuaded a British primatologist named Rosalind Hanson-Alp to take me. Back in the early 1990s, the National Geographic Society had groomed Rosalind for stardom. When Rosalind was not yet twenty-one, she had gone off on her own to observe chimps in the forest, and she observed them using tools in ways nobody in the scientific community had ever seen.

Rosalind was not yet thirty when she stopped applying for funding from the National Geographic Society. Shunning publicity, she nevertheless continued to work in Sierra Leone, setting up a chimp rehabilitation center on the outskirts of Freetown. She continued agitating for protection of the country's forests even after fleeing the country in 1996, returned as soon as it was safe. Her modesty alone made her so unusual in this day and age that I was excited about meeting her.

When I had called Sierra Leone from the U.S., the land lines rang into infinity, but I caught Rosalind on her cell. We quickly established that we had both been rebels at our elite girls' schools, middle-class kids who developed boulder-sized chips on our shoulders after being surrounded by girls whose mothers were chauffeured in Bentleys. This naturally led to what Joe had told me about Rosalind and the National Geographic Society.

"What's this about you being the new Jane Goodall?" I asked. "Did you really tell them to shove it?"

She laughed. "I can't stand that white woman in the jungle crap," she said. Then, more firmly: "We can talk about that when you get here."

Well, I was here, marveling at the humidity in the hotel parking lot when Rosalind arrived holding her two children by their hands. She looked, well, like Jane Goodall, only less emaciated and saintly, exuding a healthy sexual glow, part lioness and part Girl Guide.

We hugged, got into a waiting taxi, and headed to town. At a roundabout, we turned up a steep dirt road, passing a hillside littered with an astonishing mound of trash before entered the gates into another world: the First. Rosalind's living room could have been the living room of any hip young European couple. Lots of bookshelves, a comfortable couch, a thirteen-inch television too small for all but the most politically correct, artwork by not-quite-professional friends on the walls, two carved animal seats for the kids. The only signs that we were in Africa consisted of the electricity running off a balky generator and the bucket in the bathtub full of water. But from her balcony we had a view of the Atlantic so clear and close I could see a sandbar reclining like a blood-red ghost under the water.

ROSALIND AGREED to take a few days and travel with me to Tiwai, where she had worked on developing a campground for scientific researchers and ecologically-oriented tourism before the war withered all such notions. In our rented Toyota 4-Runner, we headed east. I had talked Rosalind into staying overnight toward Bo, Sierra Leone's second-largest city, which was about halfway to the island. I'd gotten the name of a high-ranking Kamajor leader in Bo. Go to a bar named Shelley's, I'd been told.

In addition to finding out more about the Kamajorl, I wanted to see the Bo School, a boys' preparatory school on the British model, Tom Brown's Schooldays with an African twist. The Bo School was the epitome of Lord Lugard's theory of indirect rule, building alliances with native elites, in this case, by educating the sons of paramount chiefs in a traditional British public school. In Sierra Leone, the Brits found a citizenry eager for education and the Bo School became the training ground for the country's political and business elite, not unlike Bentley College and the better-known Ivies in the U.S. Sierra Leone once was the region's Alexandria, or so they say, and for a century after its founding, Fourah Bay College in Freetown was the only European-style university in western sub-Saharan Africa. As for the Bo School, people called it "the Eton of West Africa."

Simply getting out of Freetown was a relief. One of the great scams of the oil industry that no one ever talks about is the sale of leaded gas to poor countries. Every city in Africa and many in Asia and Latin America are sinkholes of carbon dioxide. Freetown was no exception.

Red scratches marked the inverted sloping vees of hills, showing loggers had been in the neighborhood, but there was enough green to make us to feel better not only about breathing but life in general. We were tooling along a well-paved road when our driver, John started acting jumpy.

"Twenty-one drivers killed here," he said, pointing to a rise.

"What?" I said. Rosalind looked up from her book.

"The RUF and the Sierra Leone Army. They had seven battalions in Makeni. They stop the drivers. The Sierra Leone Army escorted them. They got to the top of the hill. The RUF jump out. They kill, kill everyone."

"You were a driver," I said.

"Yes. Freetown to Bo, twelve years."

I hesitated, then kept my voice neutral. "Why didn't they kill you?"

Rosalind caught my eye, shaking her head furiously.

She'd lived here for nearly twenty years and she knew the people and the culture. I ignored her. It was the logical question.

"We were just fortunate," he said. "It was the work of God."

We didn't say anything after that. About ten minutes later the Toyota nosed its way into another town. It looked like the others. Stalks of old buildings like upended corsets, their cinderblocks the color of yellowed tusks. Buildings burned in the war. Interspersed with these skeletal remains were brand-new mud brick houses, signs announcing the name of the aid agency that had built them.

"This town," John said. "This was a market. The rebels burn this area. They burn burn all."

We stopped so John could have a cigarette. An older woman passing by stopped to greet us. A satiny black bra peeked out from her bright red and yellow print *lappa*. She shook our hands in the normal way, then did a little number with her thumb I remembered as a Black Power handshake from the 1970s. Then she moved on. She left no shadow at midday and neither did anything else. The rainforest has been cut down everywhere. The lateritic soil was the color of curdled blood.

WAR DOESN'T GO AWAY when it falls from the headlines. Buildings are destroyed. People die, others damaged. People argue for years about what happened.

In Freetown, people were arguing not just about Taylor, but about the prosecution of Sam Hinga Norman. The Mende are Sierra Leone's dominant ethnic group and the east is their territory. Hinga Norman is Mende and Bo is the home of the largest and most effective Mende secret society, the Kamajors, pronounced "kamma joes."

"It really appeared that the RUF would be the new order," Joe Opala had told me. "Then the Kamajors just... appeared with all of the magic of centuries. They wore these garments that I'd seen in drawings from the 1400s and 1500s by the Portuguese. I had done years of research on those war garments as historical oddities. But I never dreamed that I would see hundreds of men in ranks wearing those things."

After the war, the Kamajors parted like waters. Some went home, to places like Bo. For others war became a way of life. Those Kamajors became mercenaries. Now they fight in places like Guinea or Cote d'Ivoire.

When we reached Bo, we looked for the Kamajor leader I had been told about. The bar he once frequented had closed and nobody seemed to know his name or perhaps they weren't keen on telling strangers his whereabouts.

John was chewing *kola*, the nut from an evergreen tree that has an effect like speed, and he'd been jacked up ever since we passed the scene of the ambush. He insisted on finding a Kamajor for me to interview. Dropping us off at the Bo School, he went off to hunt one down.

I'D FIRST HEARD of the Bo School when I spoke to Aminatta Forna. A former BBC producer based in London, Forna had written a memoir about her childhood as the daughter of one of the political figures executed during the seventeen-year "plague of locusts" presidency of Siaka Stevens. I was questioning her about Julius Maada Bio, one of the coup leaders called The Boys. Bio resigned the presidency in 1996, an unprecedented move that helped restore the semblance of democracy to the country. First Forna asked if he was Mende. Then she asked if he had gone to Bo. I didn't know the answer to either question. I asked her why these facts were important.

"Anyone who's anyone went to Bo,"she said in a trilling, fruity British accent I learned to recognize among elite West Africans. It was a common phrase, I learned later. "He must be Mende," she added. As it turned out, I discovered later, Bio was Mende. His father had been a paramount chief and he had gone to Bo.

Even today, the world inside the gates of the Bo School is a familiar one to anyone who has walked the grounds of a private college or prep school. The ambiance is hushed and secluded, as if the entire campus was a museum. Which it is, of sorts.

After John dropped us off, Rosalind and I clattered across the columned wooden veranda of the administration building looking for the headmaster's office. The secretary gave us the fish eye for turning up unannounced, but the headmaster, hearing the conversation, waved us in. He had a politician's shrewd bonhomie, a man of substance with a close-cropped gray halo around a balding pate and a nicely rounded belly.

Apologizing for the lack of notice, we explained that we wanted to learn about the school's history. "I went to a school based on the English public school system," I added, smiling in what I hoped was a winning fashion. "Also in a former colony."

"Very good," he said, in that fruity accent I'd come to recognize, curt but so much warmer than the British accent unsoftened by the lilt of West Africa.

I'd been pandering, of course, with the colony remark, as reporters do, even though it was perfectly true. When I thought of this conversation later, I'd recall what Jim Campbell, the reporter-turned-Africana Studies professor, had said about Americans abroad, our attempts at egalitarianism, so out of place in a society where hierarchy is not only acknowledged, but a source of pride, social cohesion, and a species of grace unknown in the U.S.

Undaunted by my gaucheness, the headmaster launched into a spiel on the school. Even though it was clearly well-rehearsed, we found ourselves paying close attention.

"When they colonized us, for fifty or sixty years, the chiefs were annoyed, the chiefs were angry. In 1896, they rebelled. They had something called the Hotash War. After the war, the British established the school. They said, for the sons of paramount chiefs and their nominees, let us offer a school for them in the heart of Sierra Leone. If you don't have a son, you can nominate a boy.

"So for fifty or sixty years, they did. The boys came from all the provinces, here, to Bo. The idea was that the fine native," – the headmaster pronounces the word *fine* with resonance – "is in the interior. Let us keep these boys in their traditional localities."

He looked closely at us. We nodded.

"They believed they were incited by Freetown," he said.

We nodded some more. The Creoles! Those troublemakers.

Before 1950, he told us, all the tutors at Bo were British. The boys wore white flannels and played cricket. Then came independence. In the 1960s and 1970s, Bo "Africanized" its curriculum. The school dropped Latin. Soccer replaced cricket.

Yet on Mondays, even now, Bo boys wear white flannels.

The headmaster told us that Sierra Leoneans who live in England still send their boys back to Bo to be educated. The school's 100th anniversary is coming up, he said.

"It's a loved institution," he said. "When you are a Bo boy, you carry that with you all your life. This is a bond from when you are very young. You eat here, you sleep here, you do the bad things together."

The headmaster walked us out to the columned veranda, where he delivered us to a teacher named Philip. Philip will show you around, he said, and I noticed that his fruity accent was quite similar to Forna's.t

Rosalind went off to try to call Peter, her husband, and I wandered around the campus with Philip. We walked across the grass to the library and peered in through glass-paneled doors.

I think I must have gasped. The boys sat in rows dressed in clean, pressed uniforms. But the library looked as if the Visigoths had been there and gone. The shelves hold practically no books; the remaining volumes lean against one another as if they, too, have lost limbs.

"They are taking a test," Philip whispered.

"We shouldn't disturb them," I whispered back.

I was embarrassed. That was the real reason I wanted to leave.

WE CROSSED the campus to the dormitories, named Paris, London, Berlin, mudbrick rectangles painted bright colors: blue, green, orange, yellow. Cheery, but the windows were broken out. Inside a boy ironed his shirt. The boys' cots so close to one another, I thought of black and white etchings of Lowood in *Jane Eyre*. Smiling, we backed out.

Concrete channels surrounded the building; an open sewer. Laundry swayed in the breeze.

"Very nice," I said.

Rosalind caught up with us. She dropped a few words of *krio* into the conversation and Philip loosened up. He likes teaching, he said, but he's probably going to quit.

"Why?" I asked.

"I make 250,000 Leones."

"A year?"

"A month."

"Isn't that pretty good?" I asked.

He looked at me as if he would kill me if I weren't too stupid to bother with.

"That's sixty-five dollars a month," Rosalind said.

"Sorry," I told him. "I just got here. Math wasn't my subject."

His face relaxed a bit. "Would you like to see the teacher's quarters?" We followed him across the baking-hot grass to a grove of tall trees shielding a mansion from the poisonous sun. Even in disrepair, the building was impressive, a three-story Victorian with touches of Carpenter Gothic. Gables hung everywhere like bats. We oohed and aahed. Rosalind took a photograph.

"Yes," Philip said. "It is very nice."

"Was it the headmaster's house?"

"I think so," he said. "Maybe."

White flannels might be all that remained of the old Bo School, eroded under successive iterations of history coming fast and hard. As we circled back to the gate, John waited for us under a tree. We shook Philip's hand. I found myself sad that I would never see him again, I didn't quite know why. Perhaps because he is a member of the intelligentsia, like me? Or because I sensed that he had no place anymore, like many of us, educated people in the humanities facing lives of penury in the U.S.

JOHN HAD FOUND US A KAMAJOR. He drove us up a dirt road on the outskirts of Bo to a small village invisible from the main drag. Chickens pecked at the dirt, children ran around. There was an overhang of quiet.

A shortish man came out to greet us, trailed by women, children and dogs. I'll call him Samuel. Samuel was in good shape for a forty-seven-year-old, a little gnarled, with a beard. He wore a t-shirt and shorts, and two bracelets of small white beads on his left wrist.

We sat on a bench near a playing field, but the crowd was pressing in and it had begun to rain, so we moved to the back porch of his house. Since he spoke mostly *krio*, Rosalind agreed to translate. A birdlike woman showed up through the rain. She told us she was the town's schoolteacher. She wore a flowered dress, which she smoothed over her lap as she sat, composing herself to listen.

"How did the Kamajors revive?" I asked.

"Rebels came to this country," Samuel answered. "Soldiers were everywhere. They were burning the interior villages. People who lived in the villages come to here, Kenema, Freetown."

"People begin to have hunger," the schoolteacher added. Samuel nodded.

"There were no Kamajors," he continued. "The younger generations started to defend themselves with sticks and cutlasses. Then a person whose family had been killed had a dream."

Because of the dream, the initiations began, in secret. An older man familiar with the traditions was the initiator.

"He brought leaves to them and rubbed them on their bodies and they were prepared to fight."

I asked for more details, but that was all Samuel would say, except that once they had been initiated, the Kamajors became immune to bullets. Samuel believed that an initiated Kamajor can pass on this power to others.

"If I sweat," he said, "if I put that sweat onto you, bullets would bounce off of you."

I suspected that he was sanitizing the initiation ritual, but he was being gracious and the situation was so public, it felt awkward to press him. I thanked him for the interview, then I stopped for a moment.

"What is it you hunted?" I ask.

"Elephants," he tells me. "I hunted elephants."

Elephants? The countryside was so denuded, it was hard to imagine any big game here. But I looked at him with a sudden understanding. He had the crouch and manner of the hunters I've known in America. A small man who can move in the bush.

As we walk to the Toyota, Rosalind laughed at something he'd said.

"He wants to marry you," she explained.

"Ask him how many wives he already has."

She translated.

"Three."

"Ha! Tell him I'd have to be the number one wife."

I was joking, thinking, no wonder he was telling me that if he sweated on someone, they'd be immune to bullets. It was quite an unusual come-on.

The laughter ended abruptly when, as if on cue, Samuel's number one wife showed up. Frankly, she hadn't aged as well as Samuel, so I could see why he was looking to increase the ranks. I shook her hand, abashed, and she looked at me appraisingly. If I were a chicken, she'd have wrung my neck. No translator needed for that one.

THE NEXT MORNING, John showed up vibrating with fear and stinking of booze. He told us the big men in the village have been threatening him. Apparently the village women complained that he'd led investigators from the Special Court to Samuel. He'd been up all night, trying to convince them of his innocence.

"You need to pay pay," he told us. "The chief he want to meet with you."

John swore he'd already handed over all the money we've given to him to rent himself a room for the night. He had no money for cigarettes. We gave him a little cash and sent him off. When he returned, he reported that the chief was out of town, but we would have to make our case to the assistant chief.

Rosalind was smoking incessantly. Clearly, she was furious at me. All she wanted to do was show me an island where eleven species of primates somehow made it through the war, a place she dearly loved, where biologists are trying to rebuild a research facility. She'd stopped in Bo as a favor to me, and now look what had happened. She was out of her depth, but she didn't want to admit it, and that made her even angrier.

The assistant chief showed up. Abdul was a well-dressed man in his fifties. We shook hands and exchanged pleasantries. He asked if I was enjoying my visit to the city.

"Yes," I told him. "We visited the Bo School. I understand they call it the Eton of West Africa."

"Indeed," said Abdul. "Did you know I am a Bo boy myself?"

No, I didn't. How interesting.

Small wonder that Mr. Abdul's manners were so impeccable. Given his jovial manner, I found it hard to believe that we were in any real danger, but the nasty smell of adrenaline was unmistakable. Rosalind waved me off so they could palaver. That's the word they use in *krio*. Palaver.

After they finished, Abdul waved goodbye to me as he left the café, his affluent belly pushing forward through the crowd. I smiled and waved back.

"Well, what's up?" I asked, walking up to where Rosalind was, once again, furiously smoking.

"I don't know. They want us to meet with the paramount chief, but he's not around. They don't know when he's coming back. I'm going to call Peter."

Rosalind's husband is a stunningly handsome and aristocratic half-Dutch, half-Sierra Leonean actor whose uncle is the minister for this district. She didn't want to call the minister for help, because she thinks this fosters corruption, but Peter has already told her to do it.

"Peter?" I heard her say.

Just then, her cell phone card ran out, a bit like our luck. Our driver John chose that moment to arrive our table looking like someone had stuck his head in a socket. John was clearly in the grip of *kola*-fueled post-traumatic stress, which didn't impair his drive to hustle us for money. There was a pathetic air about his efforts, as if he is begging us to take care of him, but angry at us at the same time.

"Let's just go," I said.

We were supposed to look at monkeys and goddammit, I was determined to see them.

AS THAT GREAT American philosopher Steve Miller once sang, *You know you got to go through hell before you get to heaven.*

Since we'd left Bo, driving had become an excursion to hell. The roads weren't that bad, rutted mud perfectly navigable with the Toyota 4-Runner we'd rented, along with John, from a Lebanese mechanic's shop.

But John was drunk – god knows how he found a chance to drink in the midst of our anxiety-ridden negotiations – and he seemed to be taking out his anger, or post-traumatic stress, at the poor schmucks who walk by the side of the road. That meant pretty much everyone, including sheep and chickens. He drove extremely fast. We were passed only once, by a white Land Rover. The driver swerved dramatically, leaving us buried in a meringue of dust.

"That's how the U.N. drives," Rosalind muttered. "U.N.-funded piggery."

Other than this stray comment, Rosalind had given up on speech. She merely stared out the window. She blamed me for the whole mess and she was probably right. The least I could do, I figured, was take the steering wheel away from John so we would no longer be in fear for our lives. This wasn't accomplished without a struggle, but between the two of us, Rosalind and I convinced John to move to the passenger seat. Men will agree to anything as long as you appeal to their superior knowledge. I let John coach me over the rutted road, which he seemed to know. He called me "Student." It made him feel good.

"Teacha!" I shouted in mock *krio*. "To the right?"

"Right!" he yelled.

Sometimes he would get confused. "Right! No! Left!"

Most of the time, though, he gave me good directions.

Eventually he seemed to sober up. I couldn't quite imagine how *kola* nut felt combined with alcohol, but the effects on John had considerably reduced his already meager charms.

"You take the wheel," I said finally. The road was getting worse, and jollying John along was getting old.

"You want to drive, you drive," he said.

"I'm tired."

Rosalind roused from her sulk in the backseat.

"*You* drive," she said to John, her *krio* ringing with the unmistakable tones of Empiah. "It be *your* job to drive."

That was that.

ABOUT FOUR HOURS off the main, paved road, we reached the village of Kambama. John parked under a tree, and Rosalind waved me away, no doubt wary of any other disasters I might instigate. She joined a group of men under a gazebo-like structure. Eventually she trundled over with a middle-aged man with a belly in tow. She introduced us; he was the chief. We said our hellos and he gave his benediction. We could travel to Tiwai.

After the chief withdrew, several men arrived to greet Rosalind. Children flocked to her, but nobody begged or harassed us. We were truly out in the boonies. There were the standard mudbrick houses, women sitting listlessly in the heat on the verandah, the usual chickens. Guys walked around in t-shirts and flip flops. Many sported wool hats with little pom poms on the top. The women were dressed in a combination of traditional West African cloth and bras. There seem to be more bras in Sierra Leone than in Bloomingdale's and Dillard's combined, bras worn alone – it's hot – or with a brightly colored cloth called a *lappa* wrapped in toga style, not quite covering them. It's as if Madonna never emerged from her Like a Virgin phase.

We pile in the car and head to the edge of the village, where Rosalind introduced me to several men. Mina Conteh was a dark, fine-featured man who worked with John Oates, the primatologist who set up a research facility on Tiwai Island before the war. Momoh Koroma was the boat operator; a bit younger, with a guileless smile. Lahai Lukerlay and Alusine Kanawa Koroma were volunteers.

We left John in the care of a woman who promised to feed him and headed down a path to the river. Tiwai Island was less than a mile away, in the Moa River. The Moa's headwaters are in the Guinea highlands and the broad river divides the two countries, coursing the length of Sierra Leone before spilling out into the Atlantic.

"Are there crocodiles here?" I asked.

"Yes, crocodiles," said Minah. "Eleven feet long. Some are thirteen."

The boys let us off on shore and we walked single file down a path through the trees. The humidity was nearly a hundred percent but somehow it was not close or claustrophobic, just moist, almost sweet-smelling.

"I've been completely alone here," Rosalind said, very quietly.

MINA AND MOM helped us carry our gear to a clearing. It looked like summer camp. Half a dozen basic shelters with metal roofs and concrete floors had been constructed around a central meeting place. The larger structure had walls about four feet high, painted a color that would be called "cantaloupe" in a clothing catalog. The walls dipped up and down like the backs of dolphins. Whimsical.

"Do you know Gaudi?" Rosalind asked.

"The architect?"

"Yes. I love him. I designed that. It's supposed to look like Gaudi."

I had to laugh. "It does, sort of."

Mina and the others went back to the village and we set up to cook an early supper. All of the wood was wet. We took turns, trying out favorite fire-building techniques. Rosalind was a tepee girl. She tried and cursed. I was a box-building kind of girl. I tried and cursed.

The kindling was simply too wet, soaked by rain and unable to dry out because of the humidity. The matches were too wet to strike. The air was too wet. *We* were too wet.

"I *really* don't want to do this," she said.

"Do what? Whatever it is, please do it," I said.

"Don't tell Mina or the rest of them."

She lit a strip of plastic and the fire miraculously sprang to life.

When the boys showed up, we told them anyway. They laughed. They had put firestarter in the camping box; we just hadn't seen it.

We headed into the bush, hoping to see something before it got too dark. The trees were young and stick-like; loggers in the Pacific Northwest would call them "pecker poles," a lady-like phrase I shared with my guides The forest had been cut down at least once, Rosalind said, but several of the monkey species thrive in clearings. As she spoke, a high-pitched, gurgling sound carried through the dense humidity.

"Tree squirrel," Mina said. "They follow the monkeys."

So we followed the squirrels, too, until a rustling in the leaves stopped us.

"Maxwell's tiger," I heard Mina say.

"Tiger?"

"Tiger?" he repeated, rolling his eyes. "You think there are tigers here?"

"No, no, I just heard...." But it was too late.

"Tigers!"

Lahai and Alusine sniggered behind their hands.

"Oh, come on," I said. "I knew there weren't tigers here. I just..."

"*Duiker*," Mina said. "Maxwell's *duiker*."

MINA WAS OLDER than he looked, but almost everyone in Sierra Leone is a walking paean to the age-defying properties of melanin. He started working at Tiwai Island in 1982, when John Oates arrived in Kalabama, picked him out of the chorus line and trained him as a naturalist. Oates was gone when the rebels took control of the east. The people living in Kalabama fled, and in the chaos, Mina was separated from his daughter. After the war, he spent several years searching for her in refugee camps and miraculously he found, no longer a little girl, but a teenager. This is the reason, I think, that the skin on Mina's skull is tight, the reason he is not quite so youthful once you look at him closely.

But Mina is back now, his daughter is back, and Mina is putting to use the education from Oates. Not many biologists would complain about having Oates, one of the world's foremost rainforest ecologists, as a teacher. As a boy, John Oates was enamored of the exploits of David Attenborough. As an adult he gravitated to humid places where he could study monkeys: India, the Congo, Sierra Leone. After thirty years, he came to believe that the dominant philosophy of international conservation for more than thirty years was wrong. Community conservation, the idea that local people must be involved in protecting natural areas, just doesn't work in a lot of places, especially those with a culture of corruption, he wrote in his 1999 book *Myth and Reality in the Rain Forest: How Conservation Strategies Are Failing in West Africa*.

Corruption is Sierra Leone's first, last, and middle name, so it's not surprising that when Oates wrote a book expounding his thesis, Tiwai Island was one of the places he used to illustrate his point. By the time Rosalind came to Tiwai, though, the situation was different. The country was attempting to rebuild after the civil war. And Rosalind was a different breed of Brit, although she was, in one respect, similar to at least some of her predecessors. Like Jane Goodall and the other young women protégés of the late Louis Leakey, dubbed "the Leakey Girls," Rosalind came to primatology without formal training in the field. She arrived in Sierra Leone as a rebellious nineteen-year-old fresh from her girl's school in England and with an Africa-sized chip on her shoulder. She looked like Kate Winslet and in her younger days, could act like Courtney Love coming off a binge if handed the right provocation. As her firestarting ability testifies, she wasn't anyone's idea of a Girl Guide, the British version of the Girl Scouts.

Anyone working in Sierra Leone has to be tough, I suspected. The life expectancy in Sierra Leone is thirty-five, the lowest in the world. It is a country of superlatives, in a negative way. The United Nations Development Programme rated Sierra Leone least developed country in the world. The criteria for this rating is clearly not availability of French wine, which is abundant in Freetown. As we made our way through a bottle that night, Rosalind loosened up.

"Joe told me you came with some sort of church group," I said.

"Oh, god, no. Never. A church group?"

I laughed.

"It was just a volunteer thing," she said. "Non-denominational. We planted mangroves. It lasted about six weeks."

Her anger dissipated by our surroundings and the bottle of white wine we'd had the foresight to bring, Rosalind fills in the sketchy outline I'd gotten from Joe Opala. After the mangroves were planted, Rosalind stayed in Sierra Leone, looking for conservation work. A Peace Corps volunteer said she could help with his elephant research in Outamba Kilimi, the country's largest national park.

"By the time I got there, he was gone," she said. "It was the beginning of the rainy season and the grass was fifteen feet high. It was very rainy and I had no idea how to do an elephant survey. You couldn't see them! No one had seen them for years."

What she did find were chimps. She also found a dicey political situation. When the government established the park, officials had tried to move the people out. Not surprisingly, they didn't want to leave.

"The paramount chief was very powerful," Rosalind said. "He had strong magic. They protested and it went up to the presidential level. I saw the letter to Siaka Stevens. It said: 'They want to give us millions of dollars and move us to America but we don't want to go.'

"Ultimately, they didn't move, but there was a lot of hostility. The section chief, who ranks below the paramount chief, put a spell on the park so no one would see the elephants.

"I guess it worked," I said.

"Right. They wouldn't be able to see the elephants for ten years and they wouldn't be able to cross the river. So the game wardens were nervous about crossing the river. I knew nothing about this. I said, 'Hi! I'm here to study the chimps.'" She laughed. "I was interested in studying *something*. My sister had told me about Jane Goodall and I said, well, *that* sounds easy. I went out and camped and nobody said anything. I had found a site to study the chimps about seven or eight miles in. This park is 750 square kilometers. There are no cars, no roads, no doctor. But there was a village. The section chief was there. He wanted to know what I was doing. The villagers all came 'round."

Rosalind negotiated with the section chief. She respected him and perhaps he understood this. Her anger at the British class system matched his own; she calls him "a very forward-looking, very inspiring individual who had the balls to say: "You're being disrespectful. Come to the table and don't just tell me, 'You're moving off your land.'"

With the chief's permission, Rosalind spent the next months camping solo in the bush. One day, she noticed a group of chimps were making wooden shoes – she calls them "stepping sticks" – to walk on the spiny branches of the Ceiba pentrandra tree. Her paper on the chimps was published in an academic journal. Jane Goodall herself noticed it and alerted the National Geographic Society, which funded Rosalind's research for the next four years.

Rosalind was only twenty-two when the National Geographic Society flew her to New York to give a speech. The audience included George Schaller, a naturalist among naturalists, the head of the Wildlife Conservation Society and a main character in Peter Matthiessen's book *The Snow Leopard*, and a host of other luminaries, including Goodall.

The National Geographic executive who had invited her put her up in his apartment and once he saw her hippie girl wardrobe, insisted on buying her an outfit to wear at the banquet. Once she got to the podium, he must have realized that his efforts had been in vain.

"I basically told them they'd done everything wrong and it was time for them to move along," Rosalind said, embarrassed. "I was *very* young."

After the speech, a tall brown-haired woman introduced herself.

"She held out her hand and said, 'Hi, I'm Sigourney'," Rosalind said. "I said, 'Hi, I'm Rosalind.' That was pretty much that. I didn't know who she was."

Two years later, Rosalind stopped applying for funding. There was something distasteful to her about the attention she was receiving; she felt as if she was being packaged. And she was very young, she says now; too young for all that, really. She set up a chimpanzee rehabilitation facility on the outskirts of Freetown with African partners, and found part-time jobs where she could to earn money.

Despite her good looks, Rosalind says she was spectacularly unsuccessful with boys; she thinks she was too forthright. But at twenty-two, she had met Peter Hanson, who would become her husband. Tall, elegant, frighteningly beautiful, Peter had been living in Holland, posing for Lancome ads and acting in political theater productions, but he had returned to Sierra Leone to care for his terminally ill father. Within a month after their meeting, Rosalind was pregnant. They married a few months later.

They fled to Holland once it became clear that the fighting would spread to Freetown. Rosalind spent her time in Europe raising funds for the chimpanzee refuge. When she returned to Sierra Leone the government hired her to rebuild Tiwai Island. The rebels had burned down the island's research buildings and visitor facilities. As for the primates, they were still living on the island, but they were harder to spot, cautious after being hunted for bushmeat after the war had wound down.

Something else had changed, too. John Oates' theory was either wrong, or at least it was no longer possible to use Tiwai as supporting evidence for it. The people in the villages weren't hunting monkeys as bushmeat, at least not in significant numbers. They wanted their old jobs back. They wanted Tiwai to be a preserve.

John Oates had given Mina and the other Africans superb scientific training. But Rosalind gave them something else. The people in the villages around Tiwai call her *deamo*. *Deamo* means friend. This is something they never called Oates. The difference might be called management style.

"I didn't want Peace Corps volunteers," she said, explaining how she went about restoring Tiwai. "There were Peace Corps volunteers here before and they were good. But there's a tendency for Peace Corps volunteers not to trust staff and if staff doesn't have their confidence, they tend to stall on decisions."

Rosalind told the African staff that they had to take control. Mina and the others had worked on all the handbooks and manuals for running the island. She called a meeting, where she held up the manuals and handbooks. "I said, 'Look. You know what to do. You've already done this. It has to be you. You've got to run this. You've got to have confidence in your decisions.' After that meeting, everything changed."

She gestured toward the campground. "I come back to

this place and there's no budget, but it's clean. There isn't a scrap of garbage on the ground."

The funding for Tiwai Island ran out three months ago. Mina is the only one still getting paid. The others are volunteers. Like caretakers in a haunted house, they come to the island, they clear the ground, they stack the firewood. Only two hundred visitors came to Tiwai last year; Sierra Leoneans, a few expats, and UN workers. When I tried to sell magazine editors in America on a story about it, most refused. "I hate to sound crass," one said. "But nobody's going to want to go there."

IN THE MORNING, Momoh brought a dugout canoe. Fine sand lined the inside; the canoes were all being used to haul the sand to a clearing on the island where men were using it to make concrete buildings: a laboratory, a library, and a residence for researchers. The government has given up on ecotourism for the time being, but scientists are drawn, once again, to the island.

Momoh took the stern and I asked if I could paddle in the bow. We hugged the bank until we heard noise in the trees. An enormous dark monkey jumped from one skinny raffia branch to another. He looked like a football player, with exaggeratedly broad shoulders and narrow hips, his fur tinged with green.

"That's an olive colobus," Rosalind whispered. "These are the rarest primates in West Africa."

"Not a tiger," Momoh said. I punched him on the shoulder. He just smiled.

It was still early in the morning and the shade from the trees was as good as swimming. We reached minor rapids overhung with trees. A man in a canoe was fishing. His muscles knit up all of his body; every muscle used just in the motions of everyday life. The rapids, if you can call them rapids, were just enough to keep us interested. One of the enormous trees arced over the water horizontally, like lightning strikes in a really good storm in the Sonoran desert where I live. I thought of home and didn't miss it.

"There's something felicitous about this place," I said to Rosalind. "You know, there are certain places...."

"Yes," she said, shushing me. "We wanted you to see the river."

AS WE MADE our way back upriver, I remembered something that had happened the night before. We were hurrying back to camp because it was getting dark. The trees' white branches were illuminated like networks of veins. We heard a rustling in the trees and stopped. The rustling grew more frenzied.

"There," Mina said, placing his hand on my shoulder. One, two, three, maybe five monkeys; I could barely see them through the dusk. A conflagration of monkeys. Screeches filled the air, tree branches bent.

"Red colobus monkeys," Rosalind whispered.

"Are they fighting?" I asked.

"I can't believe it," she whispered back. "I've never seen this. You're very lucky."

Something moved too quickly through the trees and there was a terrible thump. A monkey had fallen to the ground. He must have fallen forty, forty-five feet.

We waited, but nobody made a move to see if the monkey had survived. That was the right thing to do, we all knew. Not to interfere. The monkeys were supposed, after all, to be wild.

A WEEK LATER, I visited another island, closer to Free-town, that felt like the antithesis of Tiwai. In his bestselling book *Slaves in the Family*, writer Edward Ball used records from his plantation family to track down the descendants of his family's slaves. One of those was Thomalind Martin Polite, a thirty-four-year old speech pathologist from Charleston, South Carolina. Thomalind was descended from a little girl captured by slavers in 1756. Ball's ancestors, wealthy plantation owners in South Carolina, had purchased the child on the docks at Charleston and named her Priscilla.

While on a fellowship at Yale, Joe found records showing that Priscilla had been loaded onto a slave ship at Bunce Island, a humid strip of an island a few miles from Freetown. It says something about the way slavery runs through the bloodstream of this country that Bunce, an entrepôt for slave traders, was a thriving commercial center two centuries before the founding of Freetown, the country's capital.

Joe is determined to make Bunce Island a tourist desti-nation, the way Ghana has capitalized on its slave castles. Roots tourism is a growth industry in West Africa but so far it's been restricted to Ghana and Senegal. But every Heart of Darkness has its Fitzcarraldo, or perhaps it would be more accurate to say, Werner Herzog. Joe Opala is Sierra Leone's.

I hung back watching Joe striding around Bunce Island trailed by a film crew and a gaggle of people I'd started to call Friends of Joe. For different reasons, they are also here to solve the mystery of human cruelty. In their case, it is slavery. Most of the travelers are upper-middle-class

African-Americans. A retired administrative assistant on a magazine who aspires to write children's books practices Buddhism and lives in a Washington, D.C. suburb. A mixed-race storyteller from Newport, Rhode Island recently graduated from Brown. The star of a black heritage kid's TV program that used to be on Nick at Nite, and probably still is, given the network's propensity for endless feedback loops. A large and proportionately self-important African-American businessman who tells us he is investing in socially conscious diamond mining. Doing good while doing well and all that.

The inner circle of Friends of Joe included a London lawyer named Alison, the widow of a recently deceased Sierra Leonean journalist and Ann, a retired diplomat who once ran the U.S. embassy in Sierra Leone. These two extraordinarily capable women kept everything running. Alison had met her husband after coming to Sierra Leone as a volunteer in the British version of the Peace Corps, the way most Brits and Americans get there, well-intentioned kids with sufficiently strong immune systems to withstand the climate and lack of medical facilities.

The party also included a handful of reporters who all seemed to be working on stories or books featuring Joe as their main character. Jim Campbell, the professor from Brown University, came to research a book about these homecoming journeys. A professor of Africana Studies, he serves on a committee that is trying to decide what, if anything, Brown should do about the recent discovery that it owes its existence to ship owners who profited from the slave trade. Jim is white and from the Midwest, a Yale graduate married to a white South African; a few years later, he will be appointed to an endowed chair at Stanford.

There's no doubt that the Americans who have come to

Sierra Leone are sincere, and traveling to a country like this requires commitment that is more than financial. I had discovered just how much when Thomalind and her husband Antawn, a linebacker-size guy who graduated from the Citadel, arrived at the Cape Sierra Hotel.

"She's pregnant," someone whispered to me as Thomalind stepped out of the car in red carpet fashion.

NO WONDER THOMALIND can't take it anymore, I thought, remembering her condition as I watch her sink onto a fallen tree trunk in the ruins of the old fortress on Bunce Island. The rainy season had started and the humidity felt like chloroform. Poor Thomalind, I thought, as BBC cameramen and reporters from daily newspapers descended on her for the banal quotes that made this a wholesome, inspirational story to splice in between the refugee camps in Darfur and the G-8 summit.

My impression was that Thomalind is a strong-minded but basically ordinary person who lucked into being a sort of celebrity, if you can call it luck. In this odd business of African-American roots journeys, the script seems to brook no spontaneity, much less individuality. Who wrote the script? Perhaps history itself. While African-Americans obsess about wounds that are psychological, Africans are the walking wounded. If it is glaringly apparent that African-Americans, at least those with enough cash to afford a plane ticket to Africa, have more in common with white folks like us than they have with anyone in Sierra Leone, everyone is too polite to mention it.

Something else was bothering me. What is with these white guys who make a career out of the history of slavery? In a white guilt frenzy, Joe has denounced the founding fathers' connections to the slave trade, which are more pervasive than I'd realized, and this is certainly interesting. But it's also troubling that he omits James Madison, who warned that slavery would be a "black cloud over the Republic."

The immediate problem, though, is more basic: Joe is impervious to heat. He knows way too much about his subject and I am getting cranky. Very cranky.

"Bunce Island was a weird combination of fortress, a rich man's estate, and a prison," he intones. "There was a three-tiered formal garden called the Orange Walk. This was similar to a garden at Colonial Williamsburg."

He proceeds to tell us – with the voluminous detail beloved by PhDs -- about another first for Bunce Island. "A two-hole golf course was here in the 1770s. It was built by the Scots who controlled the castle at that time. This was before golf reached England."

Ah. Yet another reason Bunce Island should be preserved: the island is a landmark in the much-storied history of golf.

In the two hours we've spent sweltering in the mid-day heat, we have circled the island. By the time we reach our last stop, the overgrown cemetery where the Africans were buried, Thomalind wasn't the only one wilting.

A reporter from South Carolina has wandered off to the edge of the forest. *He's seen a monkey*, someone whispered. I left the knot of people staring determinedly at the gravestones, trying unsuccessfully to make my departure discreetly. I was desperate for a bit of nature; anything not human, unrelated to the slave trade, the fucking founding fathers, without connection to this godawful humid country or history of any kind.

But I was too late. All I saw was a shadow disappearing into the trees.

"What was it?" I asked the reporter.

"A monkey."

"It looked pretty big."

"Maybe it was a chimp. They told me one lives here."

"Only one?"

"That's what they say."

Poor lonely chimp, I thought. As I weaseled my way back to the group, Joe gave me a dirty look.

"We're almost finished," he said sternly.

"This gravestone, you'll see, belongs to someone named Adam. He was a ship's carpenter and became foreman of six hundred Africans. It was 1978 when I found a descendant of his called Bye Adam. By Adam? Remember that island we passed on the right as we came in? I canoed over to the village on the south side. It was low tide and I had to walk through a mile of mud....."

TO BE FAIR, the history of Bunce Island is fascinating. But the climate in Sierra Leone is truly rough, particularly at this time of year. By the time she gets home, Thomalind will be hospitalized for dehydration. She will swear that if she'd known what she was in for, she never would have gone on the trip. Joe and the documentary producer will pressure here to visit Rhode Island to promote their film and she'll refuse.

Thomalind told me later that she had another reason to feel overcome on Bunce Island. Joe had taken her aside to show her a small room off the main quarters. This was probably where slave traders took the women to be raped, he said.

I had stuck my head in the room and gotten the same story from Joe. I was horrified, too. I remember having the same feeling when I watched the film *Twelve Years a Slave* much later, as if the torture I was witnessing had a pornographic tinge; immoral yet we were morally obligated to watch it because of the historic shift in point of view it represented.

I checked in with Joe later, asking if there was any documentary evidence to support his statement about that small stone room.

"No," he said. "I was speculating. I wouldn't use that in your story."

HORROR STORIES AREN'T necessary to imbue Bunce Island with foreboding. Compared to the cheery, white-washed walls of the Ghanian slave castles, Bunce is a Brontean ruin constructed of gray weathered rock and brick used as ballast in slave ships. Strangler figs twine seductively along the crumbling walls. Strangler figs tighten their grip until a building either falls or becomes dependent on their embrace. If there is a better analogy for the symbiotic relationship between Africa and the imperial powers, I cannot think of one.

When we reached the shoreline of the island again, where the slate-blue Atlantic unfurled to the horizon, I suddenly felt a personal connection to the history I had been hearing. The Hare, the ship that brought Priscilla to America, was from Newport, as were the vast majority of American slave ships. New England, where my mother's family came from and where I attended college, built its economy on the backs of slaves. It was only after the region industrialized and slave labor was no longer needed on farms that New Englanders became too enlightened for the slave business.

That old Maine boy Stephen King would recognize this place, I thought, taking a last look at the darkening trees. Joe had complained that he couldn't find anyone to live on the island as a caretaker because the locals believed it was haunted. I didn't doubt it. It was if something entered our bloodstreams that day, an infection carried on the jet stream perhaps, or borne on the Atlantic, a disease from a dark continent that may be our own.

Maybe it was just the weather. Fevers abound in Sierra Leone. The lower one-third of the country is a swamp and the rainy season was relentless. On our historical tour of Freetown, Joe repeated the legends on British gravestones with an adolescent relish: "He died in a season sickly beyond comparison in a climate pre-eminently fatal to the health and life of Europeans," read the headstone of someone named John Forsythe, Esq. "He lived for many years in India," read another. "He died during his first week in the colony. This colony was, if you recall, the place the British called "White Man's Grave."

Slavery may have left ghosts on Bunce Island, but darkness is not confined to the hearts of white men. Big men practice the tactics of British colonialists by perverting traditional institutions into hierarchies of extortion. The swamp is color-blind.

ATROCITIES WERE SO widespread that prosecuting all the offenders would turn the country into an enormous prison. But David Crane's decision to prosecute only the war's leaders was criticized by ordinary people in Sierra

Leone. "Why why dese guys they kill everyone, they still running around de town?" is the common refrain.

There were many reasons for resenting the special court, but the one most commonly cited is affection for Sam Hinga Norman, the leader of the Kamajors, who was soon to face trial. A graduate of the famous British military academy Sandhurst, Hinga Norman had been implicated in an attempt to overthrow Siaka Stevens in the late 1960s, along with rebel leader Foday Sankoh. Sankoh served most of a ten-year sentence, but Hinga Norman was never convicted. His stature was such that when Tejan Kabbeh became president in 1996, he appointed Chief Norman deputy Minister of Defense. Under Hinga Norman's leadership, the Kamajors merged with the newly constituted Civil Defense Forces. They fought the rebels back, gaining control of eastern Sierra Leone, including Bo and Kenema, the second and third largest cities in the country.

A tiny cadre of American academics and think tank researchers — an historian friend calls them mercenary groupies — claim that Executive Outcomes, South African mercenaries called in by the young coup leaders before Kabbeh's election, turned the tide against the RUF. People in Sierra Leone tell a different story. They hate the mercenaries and accuse them of spraying napalm on the villages from their helicopters. To a man and woman, Sierra Leoneans will tell you that Hinga Norman and the Kamajors saved their country.

In the beginning, it is true, the Kamajors were nice boys from villages, even if they may have eaten a heart or two during their initiation ceremonies. Like Jake LaMotta in *Raging Bull*, they thought having sex would weaken their powers, so they weren't prone to using rape as a tool of war.

By 1997, though, the Kamajors had fallen into the

general madness. Many left their villages to fight farther afield. Without the oversight of their elders and communities, they adopted the tactics of their enemies. They impressed child soldiers. Court officials accuse Hinga Norman pledging that he would have a boy from every family as a soldier -- and everybody knew he didn't mean boys over eighteen. He's also been accused of threatening to use "any means necessary" to eliminate the RUF, the corrupt Sierra Leone military, and gain control of the country. Hinga Norman, of course, was in England attending Sandhurst, the country's premier military academy, in the 1960s, just across the water from where Malcolm X was pledging to use any means necessary to make political change in the U.S., so he used the phrase advisedly.

Is Hinga Norman a hero or a villain? On the child soldier issue, the jury is out, at least among some academics. In a paper he published in the academic journal *Public Culture*, Hoffman writes that the recruitment of child soldiers is seen through a different cultural framework in West Africa. Children are not considered innocents. Because they have not been initiated into society, they are something unfinished; latent, dangerous. In the United States, we would call them wild.

"Whether they have been traumatized by the violence around them or not, children are dangerous," Hoffman wrote. "Their unfinished, not quite human quality is not pacific. It poses the risks of the underworld and otherworlds with which they are associated. Having not yet been initiated, inducted into the secret societies from which they learn the ideals of social behaviour and the techniques for interpreting the world around them, they possess a power they cannot reliably control, a power of secrecy and the spirit worlds they have not entirely left. This gives a certain logic to the child as soldier. Children, combatants say, make the best soldiers because they have no fear. They obey orders without question. They are uninhibited by moral concerns. Given the simplicity of light armaments such as the AK-47, children are physically capable of participation as soldiers. But at the heart of these justifications is a sense that children are not inherently innocent. Nothing in their nature need be overcome or corrupted to turn them into fighters for whatever cause and the most ruthless fighters at that. It may be what makes the rehabilitation of child soldiers not appear to be of paramount importance; having not yet learned to be responsible social beings, ˉrehabilitation" refers to no presupposed and valued originary state. Only initiation, even into an organization the purpose of which is the exercise of violence, transforms the child into its fully human state."

Hinga Norman himself made a statement that echoed these words, describing the recruitment of children into the militia as a civilizing process: "A lot of these kids witnessed the slaughter of their parents and were so traumatized that they were living like beasts in the bush. We had to catch them and bring them back into the fold as human beings," Norman told a reporter.

Moral relativism certainly tends to come into play when the subject of Kamajors arises. But the relativism stalls out on cannibalism and random killings. The Kamajors killed civilians, hacked them into pieces, wrapped their body parts in banana leaves and saved them until lunchtime, when they ate them. They looted villages and burned people to death. They slit open the bellies of pregnant women and impaled their fetuses on spikes. Did Hinga Norman wave approvingly from his helicopter when he saw the fetuses lined up along the road as an offering to his power (a wave like Queen Elizabeth's, perhaps) or did he remonstrate with the soldiers who were surely lapsing into their own hearts of darkness? One hears it both ways.

Perhaps atrocities can be quantified. The young man who crunched numbers for the Truth and Reconciliation Commission, the precursor to the Special Court, estimated that the Kamajors committed about ten percent of the atrocities in Sierra Leone's civil war. He has worked for the commission for the past three years and he's gone back and forth on the subject of prosecuting the Kamajors. Sometimes he feels the Kamajors should be prosecuted, sometimes he doesn't. But he believes it would have made more sense to prosecute the RUF and the military in far greater numbers than the Kamajors, since they committed the majority of atrocities. This is mathematical solution may be no more absurd than any other.

But Hinga Norman, despite his sins, did something startling. In 1999, when the RUF and the corrupt Sierra Leone army marched on Freetown, Hinga Norman could have taken over the country. Instead, he stood aside. President Tejan Kabbeh returned from Guinea and Sierra Leone was restored to a semblance of a democracy. Hinga Norman, although no one's definition of a saint, is being rewarded for this by facing a jail sentence. This is the popular conception, and it why many people, including not only Joe Opala, but also the guy selling sodas on the way to Freetown's Lumley Beach isn't wild about the war crimes court.

"Don't you think justice should be applied equally?" I asked the soda guy.

"Sometimes people do bad things for a good reason," the soda guy said. "This president, George Bush. Did he tell his people the truth about the weapons in Iraq? Is George Bush on trial? Did you put George Bush in prison?"

He folded his arms and leaned back, smiling.

"But what about Charles Taylor?" I ask. "If Charles Taylor is prosecuted, would you be OK with prosecuting Hinga Norman? Would it be equal?"

"Charles Taylor will not come here," he said.

IF ONE IS CHATTY ENOUGH, simply buying a soda or riding in a cab will reveal that the average Sierra Leonean is about a hundred times more politically sophisticated than the average American. This may have something to do with one's survival riding on which way the next coup goes, and it may have something to do with the newspapers. Newspapers in Sierra Leone are both scurrilous and smart. Reporters may mangle the language, but their colonial educations have paid off. One article was a lengthy exegesis of reform presidential candidate Charles Margai's reference to Macbeth, explaining why he wouldn't win his party's nomination at the convention.

The syncretism of British English and *krio* is almost musical. "My fans should not be mentally worried a great deal, I'm striving unrelentlessly to give them what they need, and always ready to give them the best," said singer Williemina John, popularly known as Willie J, in a Freetown newspaper. Sierra Leone's top boxer is named Baby Joe Swangbeh. Another musician, a guy who goes by the name Succulent, has a hit called Da Tumba. The word Tumba isn't hard to parse: the photo shows two girls with very cute rear ends.

But it is the combination of language and myth that one remembers, particularly the one about Johnny Paul Koroma. Like Hinga Norman, Johnny Paul was a Sandhurst graduate. He was the first officer to defend Freetown against the rebels in 1991 and his former allies in the military credit Johnny Paul with staving off a second rebel advance on the capital in 1995. Others say that Johnny Paul, who won his troops' loyalty by personally bringing them their wages, switched sides, going over to the rebels, and was paid handsomely for doing so.

Still, Johnny Paul is regarded as a hero. Everyone remembers January 6, 1996, when Johnny Paul invaded Freetown to avenge the assassination of twenty-four military leaders, including his brother, reportedly ordered by the Kabbeh's vice president, Solomon Berewa. Johnny Paul was tried for treason and held in the Pademba Road prison. When the army staged a coup in May, 1997, Pademba was their first stop. They broke Johnny Paul out to become their leader. He promptly called Foday Sankoh, the rebel leader usually referred to as a madman, and offered him the vice presidency, lending credence to allegations of his disloyalty and ruin. Nigerian troops restored order within a few months and Johnny Paul disappeared.

In 1999, the Clinton administration, with the help of Jesse Jackson, engineered the worst peace deal possible, succeeding where Johnny Paul had failed by installing the psychopath Sankoh as vice president. The Lome peace accord brokered by the U.S. allowed Johnny Paul to return to Freetown from eastern Sierra Leone, where he had been hiding under the protection of notorious rebel leader and diamond smuggler Sam "Mosquito" Bockarie. Somewhere between the rutile mine and the diamond fields, Johnny Paul found God. In Freetown, he became chairman of the Peace Commission, an honorary title.

In May 2000, Johnny Paul came out of august semi-retirement with a gun in one hand and a Bible in the other. His mission? To stop the RUF from overrunning Freetown when Foday Sankoh seemed determined to start the war again. For a brief moment, Johnny Paul ran the show. Each day on the radio, he'd call on people in Freetown to shout the name of Jesus precisely at the stroke of noon. And, hallelulujah, they'd do it. His born again friends called him JP, Justice of the Peace. Some called him JP the Prophet. Others called him The Angel.

In 2003 Johnny Paul fled Freetown after a pre-dawn shootout at a military engineering depot. Government officials said that he went to Liberia with Sam Bockarie. Not long afterwards, Bockarie was killed by forces loyal to Charles Taylor. Around the same time, Sierra Leone government officials reported that Johnny Paul Koroma was dead, too.

Almost immediately, rumors surfaced that Johnny Paul was still alive.

Charles Taylor is not the only West African big man who appears to drift in and out of corporeal existence. Many people believe that Johnny Paul, the man they call The Angel, is hiding out in the eastern part of the country, or in Liberia. Johnny Paul, the rumor goes, will return to save Sierra Leone, as he did before, marching on Freetown with his loyal soldiers. He was a brave leader who earned the loyalty of his men despite his later collusion with the RUF and trading in conflict diamonds.

This story is the Sierra Leonean version of Butch Cassidy and the Sundance Kid, or of Jesus. In one photograph, Johnny Paul is wearing a white turtleneck. He looks like a Beatle. Also white are the ubiquitous Land Rovers that belong to aid agencies whose well-intentioned workers are trying to raise an entire nation from the dead.

But there is a problem. The ghosts are legion. They are uncountable. Their stories would make you weep if you were not merely trying to survive. On weekdays they make appearances in the air-conditioned rooms of the United Nations-backed special court, where former combatants offer their testimony about fetuses impaled on a spike so Chief Norman could see them from his helicopter.

There were three fetuses. Specifics are important to the court. Officials ask witnesses to repeat the facts, over and over, as if truth has many faces, and is as hard to catch as the almost microscopic mosquitoes that find their way into the visitor's gallery and may or may not carry malaria so the whiter visitors discretely attempt to smash them.

Chasing ghosts has become the national pastime.

WE WERE in the lobby of the Cape Sierra hotel, waiting for the others to join us for dinner. One of Joe's students is there, a boy with an unusual crease in his ear. I find myself touching it; I've picked up the touchiness of the people here, which felt so foreign when I arrived.

"What happened?" I ask.

"The rebels came when I was ten," he tells me. "They wanted to know where the money was. I wouldn't tell them. They told me they would cut off my ear. I still wouldn't tell them. They started cutting it, so I told them. They took the money. Then they killed my father."

He spoke in the matter-of-fact way that a college student in the U.S. would tell you that he had gone on a canoe trip to Canada over the summer.

It's one thing to hear something in the Special Court, but quite another to touch an ear, feel the unnatural crease in it. It was so smooth and dry, I remember, and it felt so natural to touch it.

The hotel lobby was like our clubhouse by then. The

staff had gotten to know us, our foibles, our needs. Charles Black, the fulsome African-American man who does voice-over narration in the U.S., had arranged a dinner at the home of a man named Andrew, the U.S. ambassador's chef. I'd missed the dinner at the ambassador's residence, but everyone raved about the food. We piled in cars and taxis and rush through the dark. I felt feverish, and a bit claustro-phobic. I had no idea where we were; all I knew was that it was a residential neighborhood and I had no idea how to get home if I wanted to leave.

"Welcome, welcome," Andrew said, smiling. Andrew and his wife Gladys were both in their late forties or early fifties. They looked slightly Asian, with high cheekbones, light skin, a certain compactness and grace.

Food covered a long table: a bowl of seasoned shrimp, a serving dish holding a reconstituted barracuda covered with some kind of mayonnaise sauce, another bowl, this one full of wilted but tasty salad.

Several bottles of wine sat on the table unopened until we are almost through with the meal. I still felt upset by Vincent's ear and I wanted a glass of wine. It occurred to me that Gladys and Andrew might be Christians of a non-drinking denomination, but I finally worked up the nerve to ask if anyone had a corkscrew.

The wine didn't make it better. The room was close and the conversation stilted. But the food tasted great. I forgot any sense of caution and ate the salad. Andrew was, after all, the chef to the American ambassador.

"Excuse me."

Andrew's wife Gladys was standing in the small space between the dining table chairs and the couch. A young teenage girl is standing next to her, equally gorgeous, her hair pulled back, lovely cheekbones.

"Yes?"

"Are you the woman from Arizona?"

"Yes. Do you know Arizona?"

"Oh, yes," she said gesturing to the girl."Her father is from Arizona."

"He is?"

"I wonder if I might speak with you?"

Many people in Sierra Leone sound as if they are characters in a novel by Jane Austen. Another product of colonialism, the gift that keeps giving.

"Of course," I say.

We go into the bedroom. A child is sleeping there, a little boy less than two years old. Gladys explains that this is the son of the young man dressed in rapper's clothes who had politely introduced himself at the beginning of the meal before going off to do whatever guys like him do at night in Sierra Leone or anywhere.

The bedroom was small. The bedclothes were rumpled. It looked like the bedroom in a lower-class family's house or trailer in the U.S.

"This is Victoria," Gladys said, introducing me to the beautiful young girl. Demure, hair pulled back in a ponytail. One could imagine her in a gym uniform at a girls' school.

Victoria held out her hand.

"Nice to meet you, Victoria," I said.

She smiled. She had astounding dimples.

Victoria's father was a blond American from Phoenix who came to Sierra Leone to look for diamonds. He met Gladys' sister in Koidu, the diamond mining district. He left in 1987, right after Victoria was born.

"He left us his equipment to sell," Gladys explained, as if that made him a decent man, a good father. "Then the war came so he could not find us."

"I want to meet him," Victoria said, shyly ducking her head. "I have an email address."

I promised to search for him when I returned to the States. I explain that I'm making several stops first. London. Namibia. Kenya. I won't be home until the end of the summer.

"You are my sister," Gladys said.

I promised to go to the beach with them on Sunday.

The next morning, Friday, I was violently ill. This was not the normal mal de tourist. I felt dizzy. I was weak. I was throwing up more than one ever wishes to throw up. I couldn't help resenting Gladys and Andrew, both for poisoning me, however unintentionally, and for forcing me into this girl's pain.

I had to move to another hotel that day; my time at the Cape Sierra was up. Before I left, I borrowed someone's cell phone to leave a message for Gladys. The beach is out, I said. Gladys sounded genuinely disappointed.

I promised to look for Victoria's father, even though I hated the idea. Perhaps I hated the idea of disappointing Victoria, too, something I regarded as inevitable.

The only sense of obligation is personal, I told myself. I don't feel complicit in any of this. I don't own DeBeers.

I RALLIED for the last day of Priscilla's homecoming. Poor Thomalind no longer had a glazed look in her eyes; she was catatonic. A reception was held at the National Museum, a moth-eaten affair that stands in sharp contrast to its executive director, a rotund woman with cute-as-a-button features whose clothing allowance seemed higher than the museum budget. After canapés, everyone headed to a hotel at the beach.

We ate lunch on the open-air verandah. Midway through the meal, a violent thunderstorm beat against the metallic air and the waves roiled in agony. Small boats rocked in the inlet. The electricity vanished, but only for a moment. Rain buffeted the roof above our heads and the air become wondrously cool with the rain pounding down like that, and many of us felt happy; we were, after all, about to be released from the manufactured emotion of Priscilla, whose name has been taken in vanity more times than God's. I sat across from the U.S. ambassador, a New England haute WASP who served in the Peace Corps in the 1960s. I tried to imagine this bald man with his suit and suspicion of Republican affiliations as a scruffy twenty-two-year-old Peace Corps kid who smoked pot and dallied with the native girls.

After lunch, students walk onstage. A woman stands up with a microphone. I recognize her from our state dinner with the ministers ("I love Phillie!" the U.S.-education Minister of Education exclaimed, after lying about the government providing free education in the public schools.)

The woman on the stage was in her mid-thirties or early forties, wearing the loose cotton clothing in Banana Republic colors that you might see on someone in Berkeley. She wore a bright gold necklace and earrings. They looked expensive.

"I want to remind everyone that slavery still exists, from forced prostitution which exists all over the world, including the U.S., to the child soldiers coerced into battle in Sierra Leone's civil war," she said.

She stepped aside so we could watch the girls lined up across the stage. Each girl played the role of a high-achieving woman from Sierra Leone's history. One was dressed as the first woman doctor in Sierra Leone. Another is the first female mayor of Freetown. One campaigned for the right of women to travel to Mecca. Another is Mammy Yoko, which I knew only as a racist epithet, but was in fact the name of a female chieftan of the Mende, who gained her position through dominating trade on the coast in the 1880s.

The last girl to speak is dressed in a contemporary business suit that almost fits her. She was portraying Christiana Thorpe, the former Minister of Education, who now heads the electoral commission. Thorpe is considered incorruptible; a sliver of hope for the 2007 elections.

The girls take turns reciting letters they've written to Priscilla, the little girl taken into slavery hundreds of years ago, introducing her to their life and achievements. At the end of presentation, one of the girls walked up to Thomalind Polite, who had watched with a glazed expression from the corner of the stage. It had been a long week for Thomalind.

Dear Priscilla, she said, looking straight into Thomalind's eyes. *If you had stayed, which one of us would you have been?*

As the strains of a song called "African Queen" rise over the room, I tried to hide the fact that I was weeping.

Perhaps it was a long week for all of us.

Nobody quite knew what to do with themselves after the girls left the stage. I asked the reporter from the *Providence Journal* if he was going to interview the woman in charge of the girls' presentation. He told me he was planning to talk to her when she emerged from the dressing room.

I had no shame. Knowing I could get into the girls' dressing room and he couldn't, I ran downstairs. After questioning several confused hotel employees, I found the right door.

The girls were in the suite's outer room, playing with their braids and hairbrushes and jiggling their feet. The woman from the stage was frantically rummaging through her purse.

"Oh, god, I can't find my cell phone," she said.

"Would you like me to come back later?"

"No, no, that's fine. I'm a mother. I'm used to multi-tasking."

She was also a British-educated human rights lawyer.

I asked her the same question I'd asked Joe, the same question I'd been asking myself. How could people do the things they'd done to each other in this terrible war?

"Sierra Leoneans feel that there's something wrong with us because of the difficulties we've had, the wars, the upheaval," she tells me. "What do you expect when for two hundred years, you're shipping out all the kids? In my daughter's class, there are twenty-six children. What if every year we sent away ten? What does that do to the others?"

Thank god, I remember thinking. This was the first intelligent thing I'd heard on this dreadful Priscilla trip.

I liked this woman. She reminded me of my best friend, who comes from a wealthy family of White Russians who settled in Paris and then the Napa Valley. Joe had mentioned her to me, telling me she is the daughter of a minister, a notoriously corrupt one.

If we all were guilty of the sins of our parents, most of us would be in trouble, I told him, not wanting to hear the condemnation in his voice. Later that night, someone tells me she'd been removed from her post as head of the Truth and Reconciliation Commission. Money was disappearing. Lots of it.

I WAS TERRIBLY SICK. Mabindi, who ran the hotel where I had moved after the Priscilla group left, put her hand on my forehead. "You're burning, girl," she said. "You need to rest. Take it easy."

I had odd shooting pains in my legs, my head felt like it was being stabbed, and Mabindi's husband was out of town, which meant the goddamn generator kept breaking. The lights went off at eight o'clock and I lay awake in the hot dark night struggling to keep panic at bay.

I'd had the foresight to ask a former diplomat for a list of doctors, which was how I found myself bursting into tears the following day in the downtown office of Dr. Willoughby, a British-educated African with a comforting deep voice. Unfortunately the voice – over the phone -- was all I ever knew of Dr. Willoughby. He wasn't there when I arrived, even though he'd told me to hop a cab and come right away. "He's just across the street," said the nurse. "I'll send for him."

I'd been in West Africa long enough to know that I could be waiting for a long time so I managed to flag down Dr. Willoughby's junior associate, Dr. Pumba. After directing a nurse to prick my finger for a blood test, he motioned me into the rear office. A secretary was working on a computer in the corner. A magisterial desk sat unoccupied. Dr. Willoughby's, I presumed.

Against the wall, under a chugging air conditioner, was an examining table. I sat on it while Dr. Pumba did the usual poking about, looked at my tongue, and asked about my symptoms. As I ran through them, I kept seeing recognition in his eyes.

"You have malaria," he said.

"But I'm on Malarone," I told him, naming the state-of-the-art preventative I'd been taking religiously since my arrival.

"This is Sierra Leone," he said. Right. White Man's Grave. I hadn't met one single person who hadn't had malaria. Falciporum malaria. Also known as the bad kind.

"It's an endemic area," said Dr. Pumba, peering at me to make sure I'd understood. I didn't know what he meant by endemic, actually, at least in terms of malaria, but I got the picture. We walked back into the outer office.

"Your blood test is negative," Dr. Pumba said. "But we will treat you in any case."

"Good," I said.

He gave me a prescription for Arinate, a derivative of a Chinese plant called artemesia, and something for the head pain manufactured in Pakistan, which I hoped was made of opium, then sent me over to a lab a block away for more tests. A slender, neat man named John Davis who wore wire-rimmed glasses accompanied me. I hope it is not insulting to call John a fixer, which is what you call people in this country who make things happen for you. John changed money for me, a good rate, and held my hand when I became startled crossing the street, something that also happens rather frequently, where the drivers are like John, and are just as likely to aim for you as avoid you.

After two days of taking Arinate, I still felt like my head was made of cotton wool, pierced by the occasional knife thrust. On the second night, I was convinced my head was no longer made of cotton wool, but of a rapidly expanding flammable substance that was going to blow my skull apart.

I sent someone from the hotel to find a thermometer but this apparently was not possible. Nobody in the entire city seemed to have a thermometer. Everybody told me I'd be alright. They'd all had malaria, every single one of them. Every African I spoke to had taken Arinate, but no one I spoke to had completed the course of medication; they just stopped taking it when they felt better. I tried not to think that I'd contracted an Arinate-resistant strain of the disease. I was too weak to be angry at a whole country.

I knocked on the door of a female professor I'd met at the special court.

"Beth?" I said weakly. She opened the door and motioned me in. She had nicely colored red hair and she'd draped pink and orange scarves around the room.

"How *are* you?" she said.

"I'm not sure," I told her. "I'm trying to figure out if I need to go to a hospital or something."

"Shit."

We'd both read the warnings that cerebral malaria requires hospitalization within 24 hours. And we both knew there wasn't a decent hospital in Sierra Leone or even any nearby country. We were talking Medevac.

She followed me to my room, where I showed her the list of doctors. "Look, here's one who lives around here," she said, sounding relieved.

When I called, though, his wife told me he was in America. *Like anyone who's got a brain*, I remember thinking. Why had I come here, anyway?

"Cold towels," she said. "Soak them in water and lay them on your head and your chest."

When I mentioned the possibility of an emergency room, she laughed, that sophisticated West African laugh that sounded like Geoffrey Holder, only the female version.

"No, no, no, no, no. You don't want to do that," she said.

A few hours later, it happened. It was like a miracle. After the laying on of cold, wet towels, my fever broke. I could think again, more or less. I could sleep.

The next day, I still could barely make it up the stairs, but I felt better, as if I had passed through a hurricane on a very small boat. I ran into one of the maids on the landing and she asked how I was feeling.

"Better."

"Praise be to God," she said. I start to shake my head, good secular humanist that I am. Then I realized I felt exactly the same way.

BY WEDNESDAY, I managed to collect myself sufficiently to meet a man whom, I'd been told, was a fairly high-level Kamajor leader. I was hoping to do better than I had the first time around, although, I reflected, I could have gotten a husband out of that deal. Or poisoned by a jealous wife.

Joe Opala's adopted son Alpha picked me up at the hotel and we took a taxi to the house he was building. The taxi dropped us at the bottom of a hill. I was surprised that I would have to walk uphill on a dirt road and then up a steep footpath.

"You must sweat it out," Alpha told me.

I felt weak but Alpha held my hand. It felt good to be outside. The sea air moved up through the canyon; I felt it and it seemed healthy. That was its reputation, and it was why the lights of the white presidential palace glowed from the other side of the rift.

Kiki was sitting on the veranda of Alpha's house propped up on his cane. He recently had surgery, an appendectomy. I was relieved he'd lived through it, selfishly; just in case my ailment grew worse, at least I knew one person who had survived a hospital stay.

As we talked, I discovered he was exactly the same age as Samuel. Forty-seven. But Kiki was the son of a paramount chief. This is not as unusual as it might sound, since paramount chiefs often have as many as ten wives. But the sons of chiefs tend to be well-educated and confident about their place in the world.

This is true of Kiki. He graduated from college and worked for a timber company in Liberia until 1985, when he could see the Doe regime was in trouble. When he came back to Freetown unemployment was terrible, he said, but managed to find a job as a clerk. He became a political activist, helping to get the current ruling party, dominated by the Mende, into power.

"Are you Mende?" I asked.

"Of course," he said.

Joe, among others, has tried to convince me that ethnic conflict didn't factor into Sierra Leone's conflict, but there was growing resentment against the Mende, who have proved to be tenacious and powerful politicians.

Once Kiki's village was threatened by the rebels, Kiki joined the Kamajors. He had already been initiated into Poro, the secret society that sees boys into manhood. I asked him how the initiation rituals were different.

"With Poro, it is only boys," he said. "Twelve, thirteen, fourteen years old. The Kamajoh initiation is quite different."

Yes. Well. Different in what way, I asked. Let's get specific.

"You become very strong. You drink this water and you become mad. You could kill anyone, even your own mother if your mother is against you. They told us the water is from the Koran."

I doubted if Kiki believed this Koran canard, but I let it pass.

Kiki was the equivalent of a supply sergeant for the Kamajors, keeping track of food and ammunition, along with troop movements. This was an army, after all, even if the soldiers believed in a West African version of The Ghost Dance. He kept a ledger, two pistols, an AK-47, and the requisite fetishes. His first military experience was as part of the force that recaptured the city of Kenema from the rebels.

"At that time the rebels controlled everywhere," he said. "We fought for three days. On day four, they disappeared. Most of them we killed, some ran away. After that, we were told to steady our place. To secure Kenema. I was there for nineteen good days."

Remembering my first, disastrous interview with Joe Opala, I asked Kiki if he had seen cannibalism among the Kamajors.

"Of course they ate people," he said. "It was wickedness. There was a law. If you did that to any civilian, you would be killed. But people did it. I cannot call it traditional. They just went crazy."

"Why did they do it?"

"If I look you in the eye, I shoot you, I eat you, then you're my companion."

"I'm not sure what you mean."

Even as I said it, I knew this wasn't completely true. I had an almost physical feeling of familiarity with what he's saying, a feeling that didn't seem personal somehow. It was in there deep, and I had never felt it before. I remembered reading Graham Greene, how, unshackled by our self-imposed obligations of political correctness, he had characterized West Africa as an earlier stage of human existence. As a teenager, Greene had been sent to a Jungian analyst after a suicide attempt. He believed in the collective unconscious.

"If I look you in the eye, I shoot you, I eat you, then you're my companion," Kiki repeated.

"I'm not sure what you mean," I said. "Can you say it another way?"

"We're all the same," he said, frustrated.

Alpha has been listening, but not saying much. "I eat you. You're part of me," he puts in helpfully.

"Sometimes it was just because of hunger," Kiki said. "The drug, it was that, too. Your heart becomes very haughty."

Kiki tells me that he knows the Kamajor leaders on trial, not just Hinga Norman but Alieu Kondewa, called "the high priest" who performed the initiations of both adults and children. I'd seen him at the Special Court. He appeared to be a broken man.

"He's an old man," Kiki said. "Hinga Norman also is very sorrowful now. He's getting older, I think now. In '67, they took power. That was 40 years ago. So Hinga Norman must be around 70."

Kiki insists that the atrocities and indiscriminate killing of civilians occurred in Hinga Norman's absence. "He say, you don't continue to kill like that. To do things like that. You have to investigate matters. He used to warn people at times."

Like many who know the political situation intimately, including Joe Opala, Kiki thinks the country could go to war again. The conditions are exactly the same as they were in the early Nineties. Kiki said he is worried that if Hinga

Norman is convicted, it will deter people from defending civilians in the future.

"We don't want that again," he says. "We don't need that no more in our lives. Even when the great-grandchild coming, we need no more war in this country."

He seemed to be looking back on his life, the way we do at this age.

"I was political but not a fighter," he says. "I changed."

He told me that he has never killed anybody.

The conversation tapered off into silence. Then, out of nowhere, Kiki asks me a question, as if we are in a class-room. "Who do you think is responsible for this?"

"Charles Taylor?"

Kiki shakes his head.

"Qaddafi?" I guess, eager to show off my knowledge.

"It was Siaka Stevens who set the war in this country. When he took up power he dealt with people by killing them, jailing them, then releasing them and running them away from this country, including Foday Sankoh and Hinga Norman."

Siaka Stevens. The man who institutionalized corruption and "systematically dismantled civil society in Sierra Leone."

A political process, not unlike the changes I had been witnessing in my own country.

THE NEXT DAY I was horribly sick. My pajama bottoms were brown in the morning when I woke up. I couldn't keep water down, much less food. When I left the air-conditioned room I almost fainted. Outside my window, a dull sunset stained the water.

I stayed in bed on Thursday, hoping I would be well

enough to catch my flight on Friday. A taxi took me to the landing strip for the helicopter. I waited for an hour and a half, listening to a screeching *griot* performing magic tricks for an apathetic audience without, it seemed, pausing for a sip of water or even a breath. A once-pretty woman with hollow cheeks and braids sold raffia bags and jewelry made of faceted plastic beads in colors reminiscent of tribal fabrics: sweet nut brown, faux ebony. A phalanx of sleek-looking government officials arrived, dark-black men wearing *kufis*, the skullcaps worn by Muslims, women dressed modestly but in forceful colors.

The hangar was boiling hot or it might have been the fever. A hawker entered, shouting: "Bobo Bele! Cry Free-town!" Borbor Bele was a CD by Emmerson, the hottest singer in Sierra Leone. The cover had a crudely drawn pencil rendering of a hefty man with a cigar in his mouth, a stack of money in one hand, a briefcase with a dollar sign in the other, his foot firmly planted on a small fellow lying on the ground who was managing to precariously hold a tray not only aloft but also level. (*Was it a tray for food, or a tray for sifting for diamonds?* I wondered.)

"A Borbor Bele is a corrupt civil servant or non-governmental employee who steals public resources! If you are not a 'Borbor Bele' you will love the songs on this album. Help STAMP OUT corruption. Copyright 2005 Bodyguard Records. All rights reserved. Unauthorised duplication is a violation of applicable laws. Online Fan Club: www.CoPhrase.com/emmerson."

I didn't think of checking to see if the Emmerson CD was pirated, which would have been ironic, because I was deciding whether I should buy a copy of *Cry Freetown!*, a documentary on the war. *Cry Freetown!* was made by a British-based Sierra Leonean journalist and cameraman named Sorious Samora. Samora had been able to remain in Freetown after the other reporters were forced to leave. I had looked for his documentary in the U.S. but it was impossible to get unless one ordered it from his website in London, which close close to a hundred dollars. There was no question about whether this *Cry Freetown* DVD was a knockoff. The front cover was lined notebook paper and the title was written in magic marker.

"How much?"

"Thirty thousand."

"Oh, come on," I said. "I saw it downtown for fifteen."

"But you are here now. Take three for sixty."

He held out two more DVDs. One was *Ecomog in Action*. The other was labeled *Atrocities*.

"I don't want that one," I said, pointing at *Atrocities*.

"Come, come, miss. Three for sixty. Good deal."

I swallowed. "I'll take these two for forty," I said, pointing to *Cry Freetown!* and *Ecomog in Action*.

"Three for sixty."

"I don't *want* that one," I said, with an edge. Thinking, what kind of person would buy that DVD, *Atrocities*. Thinking, there must be people who get off on that, like the people who watch snuff films. A whole subculture that ordinary people like me don't know about.

"OK, OK. Fifty, miss."

"Forty," I said, taking out the last of my *leones*. "I'm walking away now."

He gave me the DVDs.

Each time the helicopter would land, people queued up their luggage in a long line like horsemen on a hill in a Kurasawa epic. Only these were merely our squat quotidian bags. When it came time for me to queue my luggage, I panicked. The helicopter did not permit hand luggage and I did not have a lock for my carry on. I had spent my last *leones* on a Coke to check my nausea. One of the sleek, wealthy men wearing skullcaps stood next to me. I looked up at him helplessly.

"I have no lock for this one," I said. "Do you think it will be OK?"

"You must buy a lock," he said.

"I spend my last *leones*," I told him. "No, wait, I think I have one thousand."

"They will not sell it to you for one thousand. Come with me."

He spoke to the seller in rapid *krio*.

"You have your thousand leones?"

I handed it to him. He handed it to the seller, who gave him change, which he handed to me.

"Thank you so much," I said.

"This is no problem," he said. "You are with the U.N.?"

"Journalist," I said. "I was with Priscilla's homecoming."

"Oh, Priscilla! Very good. I am ferrying my minister to his plane." He gestures with his head to an even more serene fellow wearing a skullcap, surrounded by women and children and men of lesser rank. "I am the undersecretary of forestry."

"You are?"

"Yes. He is the minister of forestry."

"I met a Canadian the other day who was buying timber rights," I said.

"A short fellow?"

"No, fairly tall."

"Dark?"

"No, blond," I said. "He lived in Newport Beach. He was representing some consortium. Are you in the process of selling timber? How much of the country's forest is left?"

"Are you sure he wasn't a short fellow?"

"I'm sure," I said.

"Ah. You must call me the next time you come to Sierra Leone. I will see that you are treated properly. You must see more of our country. The beaches...."

"I've been very impressed with your country," I said. "All you've been through. Strong people. Just the ordinary people on the street are far more politically sophisticated than Americans."

This was the closest I could come to confronting him about corruption. Not close at all, but he caught my meaning.

He threw back his head and laughed, one of those rich African laughs.

"That's wonderful. Absolutely wonderful. I must repeat that. Well, excuse me," he said, not meeting my eyes. "I must attend to my minister."

"Thanks for your help. I really appreciate it," I said, embarrassed by my own hostility.

I COULD NOT SHAKE the fever. I called infectious disease specialists and they would not see me even though I had health insurance. "The doctor in Sierra Leone thought I had malaria. Falciporum malaria," I said. "That the bad kind." "We need a referral," said the nurse. I called my doctor and left a message. I got a message on my voicemail. "Your insurance allows you to self-refer."

I can self-refer," I remember saying into the telephone in the steely tone one of my former boyfriends had described as Teutonic.

"We need a referral from your doctor," the receptionist said.

"My doctor's never *seen* a case of malaria," I finally shouted. "He's a Jewish guy from New York! He worked in an emergency room in the Bronx!"

Stumbling back to bed I remembered John, the fixer, holding my hand. I thought of watching the BBC in my hotel room, watching Paris Hilton and Nicole Ritchie on satellite, the electricity going out, the phone lines that worked and then didn't work, the man with malarial yellow eyes, the maid who said *Praise Be to God.*

WHILE I WAS IN BED, I tried to watch Samora's documentary. I saw a soldier beating a man in the back of a pickup truck. The man cowered and the soldier brought his stick up again and again, unaffected by his victim's terror. I had to shut it off.

Instead, I lay in bed watching the HBO series *Deadwood. Deadwood* was almost as bad. The brutality of these people, my people, made perfect sense; how could it be otherwise? It occurred to me that there was a fixed percentage of cruelty in human populations. Europeans and Americans merely had their own ways of inflicting cruelty: sodomizing infants, spraying bullets on churchgoers. Demeaning each other.

Graham Greene was deeply concerned with cruelty, which he experienced as a boy in his British public school. You could say that cruelty in its various forms are the ligaments and tendons that give motion to his writing. He came to West Africa with an open heart and no pretensions, trying to understand the world and, perhaps, himself. Like Conrad, Greene is guilty of a colonial mentality at times, but his assessment of his own society's fixation with violence is telling.

Today our world seems peculiarly susceptible to brutality. There is a touch of nostalgia in the pleasure we take in gangster novels, in characters who have so agreeably simplified their emotions than they have begun living again at a level below the cerebral. We, like Wordsworth, are living after a war and a revolution, and these half-castes fighting with bombs between the cliffs of skyscrapers seem more likely than we to be aware of Proteus rising from the sea. It is not, of course, that one wishes to stay forever at that level, but when one sees to what unhappiness, to what peril of extinction centuries of cerebration have brought us, one sometimes has a curiosity to discover if one can from what we have come, to recall at which point we went astray.

Before I left for Sierra Leone, I was in love with an artist, a handsome Texan who had won awards for his short stories and novels. He was severely bipolar, a condition he had shared with me early on, in an *aw shucks ma'am* way that negated its seriousness. I was not attuned to the danger signs; indeed, they were attractive. My mother and her mother before her had possessed them, too: hypomania's effervescent charm, the unpredictable turn to disparagement and violence, a sudden coldness about the eyes. And the art. He showed me a way to look at Picasso's brush-strokes that changed my seeing forever. But the ups and downs were too much and we had broken up before my departure.

I was still feverish when the artist showed up unan-nounced wearing a pressed and starched collarless white shirt. Apology accepted. A month later, his older brother, an economist who had been downsized by an oil company, was stabbed to death in Houston, not by a stranger but by his son, who had the family's predilection for mental illness. The artist went into shock. This didn't improve his charac-ter. His cruelty was nothing new, but now it was of piece with the stories I had heard in Sierra Leone. Images of delib-erately inflicted pain unreeled around me, and inside me, streaked, flickering images of a pirated DVD.

I am alone again. I visit the emergency room for the disease no one can name. The emergency room is the only place I find comfort. The hospital looks so sterile, the walls a glorious white, rising like wings.

Perhaps, I think, the Angel is here, hiding among the monitors.

IN 2018, international soccer star George Weah was elected president of Liberia. His running mate was Charles Taylor's ex-wife, Jewel Howard Taylor. Mrs. Taylor stated that she was going to put her husband's agenda "back on the table."

BLUE MAN COUP: HOW MERCENARIES BROKE MALI

My African husband, the man I met long after I had left the artist, complains about the stereotype of "the poor African" in books and movies. But photographs often lapse into the opposite clichés: bright African fabrics, clear cobalt skies, noble ebony skin. Perhaps this is why, when he wrote about Timbuktu, the travel writer and fabulist Bruce Chatwin was canny enough to know that the fabled city couldn't live up to its advertising. Playing against type, he described the Saharan outpost as a desolate backwater where "mud walls crumble to dust and all the color is sucked out by the sun." Whether spelled Tumbuto, Tombouctou, Tumbyktu or Tembuch, Mali's ancient center of learning and commerce had always been synonymous with the remote and exotic. Inevitably, reality must disappoint.

And yet. In 2012, Timbuktu once again stood at the crossroads of history. After the fall of Libya's Moammar Qaddafi, Tuareg mercenaries, the blue men of the desert, had seized control of their ancestral desert lands in northern Mali. Invading the three cities of Timbuktu, Gao, and Kidal gave them control of a remote region believed to contain some of the world's last unexploited reserves of oil, gold, and uranium. With the central government in Bamako suddenly perceived as weak, those potential riches were up for grabs.

After the Tuareg invasion, Mali faced an emergency that threatened to turn it into a failed state and the world's next humanitarian crisis. In the twelfth century, Timbuktu had reigned as Africa's Athens and Venice rolled into one, a vibrant city built on gold, salt, and divine knowledge. A millennium later, dusty and nearly forgotten, Timbuktu once again loomed a bellwether for the commerce and culture of empire. As French mercenaries circled like vultures around an African nation once believed to be a thriving democracy, it's disturbing to think that it all could have been avoided if Western nations hadn't made their usual mistakes.

THE STORY IS straight from George Clooney's stack of yet-to-be-produced screenplays: al-Qaida, global cocaine smuggling, and a resource-rich African country crippled at birth by the International Monetary Fund and the World Bank. The political backstory may be complicated, but the cast is rife with movie star charisma. Who can resist swash-buckling indigo-clad warriors riding camels? The Tuareg are among the worlds last remaining true nomads. The Tuareg are a warrior class, traditionally disdaining labor for sport and poetry. Roughly five million live in the deserts of Niger, Mali, Algeria, Libya, and Burkina Faso. They are Muslim, but they are mostly Tuareg. Their own name for themselves means freemen; they pride themselves on bowing to no one. Legend has it that they were led to the Sahara by a warrior queen in the fourth or fifth century. It is the men who veil their faces, in deep indigo, not the women.

Even the most blasé observers acknowledge that there is something special about the Tuareg, despite their propensity for less-than-savory practices, including slavery and smuggling. Chatwin's images are indelible: in the spectral gray backwater of Timbuktu, he saw "lean, aristocratic Tuaregs of supernatural appearance, with colored leather shields and shining spears, their faces encased in indigo veils, which, like carbon paper, dye their skin a thunder-cloud blue."

Others are less romantic.

"They're professional thieves," said Peter Chilson, a professor at Washington State University, who reported on Mali on a grant from the Pulitzer Center on Crisis Reporting. "We like that, don't we? Theres a lot of romance about them, and the way they've managed to survive in the desert is sort of sexy by living off the Trans-Saharan caravan trade as guides and raiders. The technique was never to destroy these caravans, because that would destroy their livelihood, but to bleed them as they traveled back and forth. It's the Tuareg's job and they've been doing it for a thousand years."

Rebellion is also part of the Tuareg job description, first against the colonial French and later the post-colonial governments of Mali and Niger. Tuareg revolts show up in history like tree rings: 1904, 1916, 1962, 1990, 2006 and now 2012. Rebellion may be culturally hard-wired, but these rebels are not without a cause. Because the Tuareg prized honor above all, a ferocious and successful assault on such a foe could make a French military man's career. As a result, French soldiers were particularly brutal to them, according to Bruce S. Hall in his book A *History of Race in*

Muslim West Africa, 1600-1960. In post-colonial times, the Malian government continued the tradition by marginalizing the Tuareg, who do not have equal representation in government, and whose lands lack many basic services. Dashing as they are to Western eyes, nomads are regarded as second-class citizens by the region's other ethnic groups.

Nomads are as endangered as any other free-roaming creature in the twenty-first century: hunter gatherers, desert tortoises, public intellectuals without a day job. In the 1980s, salt caravans crossing the Sahara dwindled and desertification made an already difficult way of life even more so. Qaddafi's guerrilla training camps were pretty much the only gig available for Tuareg men who needed a job.

In Qaddafi's camps, young men from remote desert outposts not only learned how to wield AK-47s; they discovered James Brown and Jimi Hendrix. Members of the Grammy-award-winning band Tinariwen started playing together in one of Gaddafi's camps. It's generally acknowledged that rhythm and blues derives from the music of West Africa, particularly Mali (Martin Scorsese described Malian Ali Farka Touré's tradition as the DNA of the blues), so there is something both tidy and poetic about rock and roll, the baby of the blues, to paraphrase Muddy Waters, retracing its earlier journey to reach desert rebels.

After serving their time in the Malian military, Tinariwen's members decided they weren't gonna study war no more, trading their AK-47s for electric guitars. But for most graduates of Qaddafi's guerrilla training camps, war was their only trade. Tuareg fighters served as the backbone of the Libyan leader's militia, and when his regime fell in the summer of 2011, several thousand veteran Tuareg fighters suddenly found themselves unemployed. Their working capital consisted of high-end armaments liberated from Qaddafi's arsenal: mortars, antitank and antiaircraft weapons. In early 2012, they bore down on the north, declaring themselves standard-bearers of a new liberation movement, the MNLA, or Mouvement National Pour la Liberation de l'Azawad, Azawad being the Tuareg name for northern Mali.

FOR *NEW YORK TIMES* REPORTER ADAM NOSSITER, the insurrection's lineage merged the long Tuareg history of rebellion with the pan-African ambitions of Qaddafi, an inspirational figure as well as a disruptive force in sub-Saharan Africa for much of the twentieth century. "In life, he delighted in fomenting insurgencies in the African nations to the south. And in death, Col. Muammar el-Qaddafi is doing it all over again," wrote Nossiter.

If nothing else, Libya's vast oil wealth gave Qaddafi the resources to train a professional military. Faced with the Tuareg fighters, the underpaid and ill-trained Malian army quickly lost control. The army's most humiliating moment came when the Tuareg overran one of its military bases. The reason? Government soldiers had run out of ammunition, according to Jeremy Keenan, a professor at the University of London's School of Oriental and African Studies.

With the Tuareg offensive weakening the Bamako government's already shaky hold on the country, a cadre of junior officers staged a coup in March, installing a young officer, Captain Amadou Sanogo as the country's leader. While Sanogo was trained in the U.S., by most accounts, the coup was not backed by outside forces. Whatever its roots, far from strengthening the Malian military, the post-coup disarray gave the rebels an opportunity to press their advantage. With two of the north's major cities already under their control, they advanced further into the desert. Timbuktu fell on the first of April.

Spokesmen quickly made their demands, including recognition of an independent Tuareg state. Just as quickly, the African Union and the U.S. Department of State rejected their demands, contending that national boundaries, even though they were drawn by colonial powers, take precedence over ancestral land claims. Privately, even MNLA sympathizers, including Tuareg in the U.S., noted that the group had no formal structure or defined leadership and would be unlikely to govern effectively. The best-case scenario was a power-sharing agreement guaranteeing Tuareg leaders full participation in the Malian government. As one Tuareg said: "There's a saying we have: Ask for more than you can get, and get what you want."

As the situation in the capital city of Bamako became increasingly chaotic, hope for a quick settlement receded. Under economic sanctions and the threat of military action by the Economic Community of West African States, Sanogo handed power to Mali's former parliamentary speaker and a presidential candidate, Diaconda Traoré, with the understanding that elections would be held in 40 days if possible.

Traoré named Cheick Modibo Diarra, another leading presidential contender, as prime minister. Diarra, the chairman of Microsoft Africa, was an astrophysicist who once worked for NASA, but a newcomer to politics. Sensing weakness, the military flexed its muscles again, arresting high-ranking allies of ex-president Touré. Following an outcry, the men were freed, but as the weeks passed, it looked increasingly unlikely that the military would relinquish control.

In the north and the south, violence came and went in a call-and-response rhythm. In Bamako, a counter-coup attempt by presidential guards, reportedly aided by mercenary soldiers, failed May 1. Four days later, radical Islamists of the Ansar Dine group associated with al-Qaida attacked a Sufi saint's shrine in Timbuktu, confirming the fears of art historians and archaeologists that this century's upheaval would jeopardize the ancient city's cultural treasures.

QADDAFI'S DOWNFALL was the trigger for much of the instability afflicting West Africa from Mali to Nigeria, where a United Nations report found that heavy-duty weaponry from Libyan stockpiles, including rocket-propelled grenades, machine guns with anti-aircraft visors, automatic rifles, ammunition, grenades, explosives, and anti-aircraft artillery and possibly surface-to-air-missiles had strengthened Boko Haram and Al Qaeda. Mali's implosion was one of those unintended consequences that so often eclipse the illusory goals of Western intervention. As Bajan Ag Hamatou, a lawmaker from Ménaka, complained to Nossiter of *The New York Times*: "The Westerners didn't want Qaddafi, and they got rid of him, and they created problems for all of us. When you chased Qaddafi out in that barbaric fashion, you created 10 more Qaddafis. The whole Sahara-Sahelian region has become unlivable."

Western meddling was not new to the region, and, without soft-pedaling Mali's internal problems, there's little question that the country's fragility was not entirely of its own making. With onlookers straining to track who's on first in Bamako, it was easy to overlook the obvious question:

What kind of army runs out of bullets? The answer is simple: an army in a country saddled with $3 billion in debt, corruption, and cronyism.

Vijay Prashad, the George and Martha Kellner chair in South Asian history and professor of international studies at Trinity College in Hartford, Conn., recounts a tale that sounds familiar to anyone familiar with Africa's recent history. A socialist leader striving to make an African country self-sufficient in the 1970s is replaced by a leader friendly to the West. Buying into neoliberal capitalist notions of "development," Mali's borrowed from the World Bank and the International Monetary Fund (IMF), piling on debt that Mali found impossible to pay.

By the end of the 1980s, according to Prashad, Mali had become the test case for structural readjustment, the privatization initiatives and public-sector cutbacks imposed on debtor nations by institutions like the World Bank and IMF.

Take note, Americans: Mali's story could be America's, if tax-cutting, anti-government Republicans like Paul Ryan have their way.

Want to see a postcard from the future? By 1989, Mali was spending 100.8 percent of its gross national product on debt service. By 1992, Mali's debt had escalated to $3 billion. *New York Times* reporter Howard French quoted an associate of Mali's president: We service our country's debt on time every month, never missing a penny, and all the time the people are getting poorer and poorer.

Mali's president begged the United States and Europe to either forgive the debt or restructure it, Prashad wrote, but Washington held fast. George Moose, Clinton's assistant secretary of State for African affairs, cited moral hazard, the notion that bailing someone out will cause them to take more risks. There was an infantilizing aspect to the argument but it did seem to work that way, if the government bailout of the U.S. financial industry was any guide.

In Mali, where there was less fat to trim, the consequences were immediate and they were stark. Government salaries could not be paid. Ammunition could not be purchased. Forced privatization hurt the cotton market and decimated fragile farming in the arid north. People got poorer, and hungrier.

There is a caveat. Without minimizing the damage of international lending policies, it would be both patronizing and inaccurate to hold the West entirely responsible for Mali's troubles. The marriage of development aid and corruption is highly combustible. David Gutelius, who worked in the region as a development economist, criticizes international development programs for lining the pockets of Mali's politically connected elite without improving conditions for the poor. According to Gutelius, the lack of viable economic alternatives and government services in the northern desert was the result of the Traoré government's cronyism. Corruption and tribalism fostered successive Tuareg rebellions.

At the same time, Mali's desperate financial situation left the country, which is 80 percent Muslim, dependent on Islamic nongovernmental organizations and missionary groups, including those dedicated to a purer Islam.

THE BELIEF that ungoverned spaces such as the Sahara provide safe havens for terrorist groups resulted in several major changes in U.S. foreign policy after 9/11. In 2002, the U.S. set up the Pan Sahel Initiative, renamed the Trans-Sahara Counterterrorism Initiative in 2005. The aim was to train the military from seven willing Saharan countries and partner with them to fight terrorists. In 2007, the Pentagon set up a separate command structure for Africa, signaling a new focus on the continent.

Initially, the Trans-Sahara effort received $500 million in funding over a five-year period. Most of the money was for military training and weapons, but a portion was dedicated to a hearts and minds campaign: revising textbooks, paying for schools teaching a tolerant ideology and running moderate radio stations, according to Vijay Prashad, a professor of South Asian history and international studies at Trinity College in Hartford, Conn.

But a gap in funding in the program's second year excised the "hearts and minds" part of the strategy. Counterterrorism dollars flowed to the Bamako government, and the rebel-held north remained without basic health and education services. In radio programmes and sermons, Tuareg leaders, as well as young Fulani, Bellah and Songhai scholars from Timbuktu, Gao and Mopti, placed blame for local conditions to the U.S. and its Malian sycophants, David Gutelius, a development economist who worked in the region, wrote in ISIM Review in 2006.

According to Gutelius, this is just one of many ways that U.S. counterterrorism efforts have backfired.

IT'S BECOME a truism to say that border zones comprise a third country, shifting ground where cultures hybridize. With power and money concentrated in the south of Mali, the northern Sahara region has largely been left to itself or, rather, to neighboring Algeria, a richer country whose infrastructure is closer to the Malian desert. In the past, the Malian government kept the Tuareg from rebelling by giving them military jobs while continuing to neglect the region's infrastructure, including schools and basic medical facilities. The shortcomings of that Band-Aid strategy became glaringly apparent when as many as 1,500 Tuareg deserted the Malian army and joined the MNLA rebels.

The irony is that Mali's economy had been booming, in part because of gold mines mainly concentrated in the south. According to Peter Chilson, improvements in Mali's transportation system helped fuel economic growth, but the three main cities in northern Mali: Gao, Kidal and Timbuktu, remained difficult to reach from southern Mali and Bamako. With bad roads and little government infrastructure, most day-to-day necessities come from Algeria. But there are no formal trade agreements in place between Algeria and Mali, so the only way to obtain these items is via smuggling.

Smuggling is a time-honored tradition in the Sahara, with social and even spiritual overtones. But in the 1990s, smuggling in the Sahara became part of the global economy as the trade shifted to smuggling cigarettes into Europe via Italy. Soon the trade grew more hardcore, as drugs, weapons, and people became the commodities.

For the U.S., it had been difficult to distinguish smugglers from terrorists. This wasn't just the usual American thickheadedness; you truly needed a scorecard to keep track of the shifting alliances. But by the early 2000s, many of the emirs who headed smuggling operations were affiliated with the GSPC (the Salafist Group for Preaching and Combat), an Islamist militia. The group was fairly low profile until 2003, when Amari Saïfi (aka Abdelrezak el-Para) kidnapped 32 European tourists in Algeria's southern desert massifs. After the German government reportedly ransomed the hostages, the perpetrators were tracked down in Chad with logistical support by U.S. military forces.

This dramatic four-country chase across the desert helped build support for American involvement in the region. Lost in the excitement were the assessments of experts who described the GSPC as primarily a business operation. Thats not to say the group had no political ties, but these appear to have been strategic and commercially motivated, as cigarettes moved north, guns traveled south. The nicknames of one of the GSPC's best-known leaders, Mokhtar Belmokhtar, speak volumes: One-Eye, because he lost an eye fighting in Afghanistan in the 1990s, and Mr. Marlboro.

The best evidence that the GSPC had drifted from its revolutionary roots was the formation, in 2007, of a GSPC splinter group called AQIM (al-Qaida in the Islamic Maghreb). The group had reportedly allied itself with the original al-Qaida at the personal invitation of Osama bin Laden. On April 4, the French foreign minister warned that the groups involvement in the Tuareg MNLA rebellion could strengthen the terrorist threat worldwide, and urged countries throughout the region to take action.

The reality is that in impoverished, marginalized places with weak governance, people will support virtually anyone who provides jobs, schools, and health care, whether through legal or illegal means. Salafist preachers from Pakistan arrived in northern Mali in the 1990s, making inroads in both the GSPC and among some Tuareg. But longtime observers believe that the real business of purported Islamic extremists is, in fact, business: controlling the Trans-Sahara trade.

IN THE TWENTY-FIRST CENTURY, the Sahara trade consists of smuggling cocaine, human trafficking and, increasingly, kidnapping. In 2009, a Boeing 727 crash-landed in northern Mali, where an undisclosed but by all accounts significant quantity of cocaine was offloaded. The smugglers, who had flown from Venezuela, torched the jet. The burned hulk was found abandoned in the desert.

This watershed event was a signal that the days of cramped Beechcraft three-seaters were gone. Drug smugglers have gone global, running fleets of transatlantic ships and corporate and commercial jets, and West Africa is a international crossroads for the cocaine trade. The United Nations Office on Drugs and Crime estimated that in 2007, 40 to 50 tons of cocaine was funneled through West Africa, worth an estimated $1.8 billion at European wholesale prices. But the real volume is believed to be much higher. Perhaps the best gut-level index is the construction industry in the Senegalese capital Dakar, where the economy is nose-diving, yet white concrete mansions are rising along the coast at record speed.

Along with Nigeria, Guinea and Guinea Bissau, Mali is a route for shipments from the transit hub of Dakar to Europe. As much as 80 percent of the cocaine seized in Western Europe is believed to have crossed Mali. Drugs and politics are intertwined on both sides of the equation. Colombia's rebel group FARC trades cocaine for arms, with the reported involvement of government figures. In Mali, the trade is dominated by emirs like Iyad ag Aghaly, one of AQIMs leaders. Keenan is sometimes accused of being a conspiracy theorist, but he has spent considerable time on the ground in the Sahara. The professor believes that Aghaly is partners in the cocaine trade with Algeria's secret police.

The Algerian government explained its army's presence in the north of Mali in December as an effort to combat

AQIM, but Keenan says that the Algerians were on the ground to protect their stake in the drug trade from the Tuareg MNLA.

Indeed, the MNLA has said that the reason why AQIM is protected by both Algeria and Mali is because AQIM is a cover for the massive billion-dollar cocaine trafficking industry controlled by rogue elements in the political-military elites of both countries, according to Keenan, who called Mali a "narco-state."

To add to the intrigue, economist Gutelius reported rumors that the Malian government had made deals with radical Islamists in the north to suppress the nationalist element of the Tuareg movement.

The drug trade remains lucrative, but Gutelius said that the unintended consequence of a U.S.-backed crackdown on the drug trade was a shift to kidnapping. Daniel Benjamin, coordinator of counterterrorism at the U.S. Department of State, agreed. After AQIM claimed responsibility for kidnapping four Europeans in 2009, Benjamin wrote that the group was financially strapped, particularly in Algeria, and unable to reach its recruiting goals, and as a result, was concentrating on kidnapping Westerners. Since 2009, kidnappings have decimated tourism in the Sahara, yet another blow to the region's above-ground economy.

TWO OF THE victims were not mere tourists. Philippe Verdon and Serge Lazarevic might be described as two characters in search of a coup, French nationals variously described as mercenary soldiers, or adventurers who claimed ties to mercenaries. Verdon, who once ran an airline in Madagascar, claimed to know the legendary mercenary Bob Denard. Prior to arriving in Mali, he was last seen with an Israeli general allegedly discussing the use of mercenaries in Libya.

Lazarevic, who reportedly has ties to French security services, is believed to have recruited mercenaries for former Zaire President Mobutu Sese Seko in the Nineties and is wanted for questioning in Kosovo. Last November, the two men arrived in Mali, ostensibly to work on a cement project, and were promptly kidnapped by AQIM members.

France retains a proprietary interest in many of its former colonies. The U.S. is reportedly stepping back, providing support but giving the lead to France when it comes to Mali. Although there's no evidence that Verdon and Lazarevic were representing France, there is more than a whiff of an old Frederick Forsyth potboiler in their travails.

But the majority of AQIM's kidnapping victims have been bystanders to the Sahara's intrigue: aid workers, tourists and missionaries. The group is implicated in the deliberate killing of at least 10 European civilians and the kidnapping of half a dozen Europeans.

"I think its part of this larger story of increased competition in the Sahel," Gutelius said. "You've got higher-priced commodities. Instead of guns and cigarettes, you've got people. When risk goes up, so do prices."

The shift to kidnapping alienated some of the traditional emirs, notably Belmokhtar, according to David Gutelius.

"When the game changed, the balance of power among the smugglers in the desert shifted, too," he said.

Are the emirs of the Sahara criminals or revolutionaries? A little bit of both. Stephen Harmon, a professor at Kansas Pittsburg State University and a specialist in West African Islamist history, is convinced that the GSPC and

AQIM are more concerned with their illicit business than with overthrowing the Algerian government or jihad. In the Concerned Africa Scholars Bulletin, Harmon argued that the U.S. and Algeria have exaggerated the threat posed by these groups to justify an American military presence and, in Algeria's case, the continued rule of an authoritarian government.

Harmon's analysis will sound familiar to anyone who has followed U.S. foreign policy in Latin America, where for decades the U.S. propped up repressive dictatorships to buttress its sphere of influence. In Mali, and in Africa generally, U.S. counterterrorism efforts have bolstered the arsenals of unpopular, corrupt, and repressive regimes, inadvertently creating even more support for terrorist organizations.

The real problem for the U.S. may be that there are no white hats in the desert. But if anyone is sympathetic in this scenario, it may be the Tuareg. Alliances between the Tuareg resistance and radical Islamists in northern Mali appear to be tactical and easily broken, and tensions between these groups outweigh their commonalities. The overarching goal of most Tuareg is simply to survive, while preserving their culture. And the biggest threat to the Tuaregs survival is not Mali's current political predicament, but oil, gold and uranium.

At the crossroads of the Sahara, it comes down to money, for Islamic freedom fighters and Great Satan Americans alike, and the economic stakes in Mali, particularly northern Mali, are enormous. It may be one of the worlds poorest countries, but Mali is also the third-largest producer of gold in Africa. Canada is the major player, with at least two corporations, Iamgold and Avion Gold, engaged in mining operations in the south. With gold reserves waiting to be tapped in the north, Mali was selected by Canada in 2009 as one of six African countries of focus for Canadian aid.

There are likely to be even bigger stakes in oil, uranium and bauxite. Exploratory drilling showed promise in the norths Taoudeni basin, at Mali's border with Mauritania and Algeria, as early as the 1970s. Algeria's national oil company, Sonatrach, and Canadian owned Selier Energy bought significant stakes in the region in 2007, but those projects are on hold because of the recent instability.

Oil tends to get most of the attention, but France is heavily dependent on nuclear power and already has a major interest in uranium mining in the region. Its no coincidence that the Bush administrations pretext for the Iraq War involved a false story that Saddam Hussein was importing uranium from neighboring Niger, where the French company Areva has mined more than 100,000 tons of uranium since 1968, most of it going to power the country's 58 nuclear reactors.

Niger is to the nuclear industry what Saudi Arabia is to the oil industry, said Okey Iheduru, a professor at Arizona State University who consults on risk assessment. It certainly hasn't been lost on the MNLA fighters that in Niger, uranium mining takes place on traditional Tuareg land, and Tuareg miners, some of whom begin working as young as 11, are exposed to high levels of radiation.

It sounds like a graffiti by Banksy, or perhaps a line from 1984, but with massive and inevitably, poorly regulated mining and oil drilling on the horizon, the motto for the Tuareg insurgents could be: Fear Peace.

Instability may keep the oil and uranium companies at bay, but at a price. Over the past decade, drought has made life in the Sahara increasingly difficult. Baz Lecocq, a lecturer at Belgium's Ghent University and a well-regarded commentator on the Sahara, recently wrote of an impending crisis. This year, there is no food surplus and no pasture left to sustain people and herds through the heat in northern Mali, he wrote on the website African Arguments on March 30.

"Those who have not already fled the fighting in early January will have a very hard time getting out now. The drought of recent years is building up to a hunger season that could well become a famine on a disastrous scale."

If you think Bamako is hot in April, Lecocq warned, try Kidal in a shady noon at around 130 degrees Fahrenheit.

If we have learned anything, it is that these crises are neither natural nor inevitable, but the product of egregious mistakes repeated so consistently that starvation in Africa has become our era's ritualized tragedy, a performance of suffering that offers those in the West an emotional rush but no challenge to understand how the debacle occurred or to face the roles their own nation's play in it. In the face of an uncertain future, the persistence of Tuareg spirit is both comforting and disturbing, a harbinger of an increasingly borderless world that is not ungoverned, but whose rules and boundaries may be determined by varieties of free trade that Milton Friedman never imagined.

"We are military artists!" Abdallah Ag Alhousseyni, Tinariwen's lead singer, told a journalist from Algérie News. "Today, if we see that our brothers need fighters rather than musicians, we will go to the front, because we are always ready to answer the call of the preservation of our land, our values and our culture. This is what we do through music, and we will do it again with arms!"

FOUR

THE FAILED STATE CHICK

When photojournalist Camille Lepage was killed in the Central African Republic in 2014, a colleague paid her the ultimate insider's compliment, calling her "this very discreet yet inquisitive and incredible journalist" in the tradition of Corinne Dufka.

Dufka is the most famous journalist you never heard of, a quiet iconoclast who belies the tradition of the trench-coated foreign correspondent who boasts about the bullets he's dodged and the dictators he's known, a club that until recently has been mostly male. Dufka, for example, would never mention her MacArthur "Genius" grant, although she's competitive enough to be annoyed that she missed out on a Pulitzer because her photograph were deemed too negative.

That particular photograph showed Liberian soldiers executing a man. There was talk that the jury felt uncom-fortable because Dufka photographed the execution rather than stopping it. "I had talked people out of shooting someone many times," she says. "I wasn't fast enough that time, so all I could do was pick up my camera." A photograph of Boris Yeltsin dancing with showgirls won instead.

Dufka's photographs are powerfully evocative and sometimes unbearably painful, but her friends call her "fun" and even a brief acquaintance confirms that she has a goofy sense of humor. But dancing girls are not her schtick. With a master's in social work from the University of California at Berkeley, she began her career as a volunteer social worker with the Lutheran church in El Salvador. Finding church workers a sanctimonious bunch, she bonded with Salvadoran reporters and the foreign press covering the war.

Dufka's father, an aerospace engineer, was one of those amateur photographers who dreams of making his hobby a profession. Before she took off for El Salvador, she bought a camera and while using it to document human rights abuses for the church, she says, "I just sort of fell in love with the medium." Hoping to switch careers, she bought a raft of books about photojournalism. The work of W. Eugene Smith affected her the most, she recalls.

"I remember really clearly sitting in my kitchen in El Salvador when I was thinking of making this transition and looking at these pictures of napalm victims, tears rolling down my face," she said. The effect of Smith's images must have been profound, because Dufka's photographs, in their raw emotion, are closer to Smith's than to her other predecessors.

Dufka apprenticed herself to Roberto Nava, a Salvadoran photojournalist working for Reuters. After Nava was killed by the Salvadoran army, she landed his gig with Reuters. She was not unaware of the irony, or the debt she owed him. From Salvador, she moved on to Bosnia, where she was wounded in the face by shrapnel, scars that are barely visible now. By the time the war in the Balkans ended, Dufka was well-established in her profession. She joined the Nairobi bureau of Reuters, where the "dirty wars" in West Africa became her beat.

Any journalist needs to put emotions aside, not only in the interests of fairness but to meet deadlines. After a while, detachment becomes reflexive and war reporters often suffer the greatest harm. In 1998, Dufka began to question not the psychological toll, but the morality of her work. She was in Kigali when Al Qaeda bombed the U.S. embassy in Nairobi in 1998. Before the car bomb went off, the terrorists had thrown a grenade, shattering the glass in a nearby office building. Workers who had run to the windows to see what the commotion was about were blinded by the shards of glass.

Dufka's mother and sister were both legally blind; her mother had suffered from depression as a result. Dufka, waiting for a plane to take her to cover the fighting in the Democratic Republic of Congo, had the unusual — for her — experience of watching the news on television instead of covering it. Suddenly, all the emotions she had suppressed, channeling them into her photography, rushed to the surface.

" I completely lost it," she says. "I think it was because I was at a remove, in this hotel room, so I had the time and the space to have those feelings. I had been so angry and distraught, realizing that I had missed the story that would get the most attention from the world. I hadn't stopped to think about the Kenyans who were hurt and killed. But having the family history of blindness with my mother and my sister made me realize that I'd been behaving in a way that was devoid of humanity."

Shortly afterwards, Dufka landed a job Human Rights Watch. She has remained with the organization for nearly twenty years, including a year's leave of absence when she put her reporting skills to work for the Special Court for Sierra Leone, investigating war crimes and human rights abuses.

When I talked to her, Dufka was researching the radical group Boko Haram in Nigeria. The group's kidnapping of nearly 300 schoolgirls had captured the world's attention. But Dufka was concerned that Americans were missing the real story. According to Dufka, this is the story of so-called failed states, no matter which continent they are on.

The short version is a paraphrase of James Carville's immortal explanation for the defeat of the George H.W. Bush and presidential elections in general: *The economy, stupid*. But when it comes to the withering away of civil society?

It's corruption, stupid.

SZ: Let's start with the girls kidnapped by Boko Haram in Nigeria. What is the press getting wrong?

CD: They're not getting anything wrong, it's just an incomplete picture. The abduction of the girls is, of course, an extremely grave crime. But to focus exclusively on the girls lacks an appreciation of the wide and systematic crimes committed by Boko Haram in recent years, and also by the Nigerian army since the state of emergency was declared almost a year ago. There have been scores of attacks on towns and villages, and well over a thousand people killed, hacked to death, dragged out of their cars and murdered. Scores of boys and young men have been killed in school attacks.

SZ: Have schools been a particular target?

CD: The name "Boko Haram" means Western education is sin. They have opposed Western education from the very beginning, and schools are among their main targets. They've attacked and burned schools of all different levels, from primary and secondary schools to technical and academic colleges. As recently as March, forty-three students were hacked to death in a government college. The abduction of the girls is just one of many attacks against educational institutions.

SZ: What has Nigeria's government done?

CD: In response to death threats by Boko Haram, the Nigerian army has set up widespread and arbitrary detention, in horrible conditions that have led to the deaths of many men without court proceedings to determine their guilt or innocence. There could be a campaign "Bring Back our Boys" led by the mothers of boys and men who are arbitrarily detained. Many have died. We met with numbers of these women. It was heartbreaking. Both sides have committed violations. It's important to keep that in mind.

SZ: Is there something unique about Boko Haram?

CD: Boko Haram seems to be a disturbing fusion between the Sierra Leone rebel movement in the 1990s and al-Qaida. The tactics used in Sierra Leone were designed to terrify. The RUF—the Revolutionary United Front—compensated for their low numbers by terrifying the population and swelling their ranks as people joined them out of fear. Boko Haram is also using sheer terror to intimidate and ultimately control the population. They profess to be grounded in Islam but an Islam that, as many scholars have pointed out, is against the principles of Islam.

SZ: You've worked in a number of countries known as failed states. What have you learned about the causes of state failure?

CD: Rapid population growth is one factor. Some West

African countries have the highest population growth in the world. No country can keep up with that. Climate change, desertification, economic factors and, lastly, endemic corruption. But Nigeria is not a failed state. It has very strong institutions, a strong central government, a strong media, a strong electoral process. The problem with Nigeria is not that it's a failed state but a deeply corrupt state. Boko Haram started out years ago preaching against corruption. Followers gravitated toward a group that seems to offer them more than the state does.

SZ: Boko Haram has been expanding its violent activities for several years. We weren't paying much attention to Nigeria before the girls were kidnapped, were we?

CD: Not enough. We shouldn't only zoom in on places where the conflict is already surfacing. The fact that Mali, which essentially collapsed two years ago, was considered a success story by the West is an indictment of development policy. It's a culture of low expectations. As long as there are elections that are not characterized by extreme violence, as long as there is not overt armed conflict, then a country stays out of the problem category.

SZ: What are the signs we should be looking for?

CD: The growth of fundamentalist religion happens for a reason. In Africa, it's rooted in the failure of ethnic and tribal structures, as well as the government, to address the basic needs of the population: health, education, clean water. I would include the opportunity to flourish as necessary for a healthy society. Into that vacuum creeps what I call the Meddlers. In past decades the Meddlers were rebel groups like the ones we saw in Sierra Leone and Liberia. They were supported by Moammar Qaddafi, Blaise Compaoré of Burkina Faso, and others who benefited from resource exploitation by the Meddlers. The modern day

Meddlers are drug traffickers from South America, who are using West Africa as a route to sell their wares in Europe, as well as religious fundamentalists.

SZ: Critics are charging that #bringbackourgirls is an excuse to expand the U.S. military presence in Nigeria, one of the world's largest oil producers.

CD: Business interests are already involved. I think the U.S. is more concerned about the security implications.

SZ: Speaking of security, how closely allied to al-Qaida is Boko Haram?

CD: The extent to which they are allied with al-Qaida isn't really clear. That's a work in progress; it's gone back and forth.

SZ: Boko Haram has been fairly tough to characterize until now, partly because it's been too dangerous for journalists to travel to the north. In general, covering wars is more dangerous now. Is that why we're becoming fascinated by the people who do this work?

CD: It's a manifestation of the cult of personality that infects our society. But it's true that the conflicts are getting more dangerous.

SZ: Is there a personality type for people attracted to the work?

CD: They're all fucked up [laughs]. No, not really.

SZ: Samantha Power called herself "the genocide chick," which helped make her a star. Aren't you the original genocide chick?

CD: Wouldn't Martha Gellhorn be the original genocide chick?

SZ: So you're the failed state chick.

CD: I'm the failed state chick.

SZ: It's a great sound bite, the chick thing, but what's the reality? When Camille Lepage died, *The New York*

Times compared her photographs to yours because of their emotional impact. We need to be careful about attributing differences to gender, but is there something different about the way women cover war?

CD: It was very sad, her death. But in terms of differences, I don't think so. I really don't. I've never bought into that. Women do not have a monopoly on paying attention to emotional issues.

FIVE

THE WAR ON SHANGRI-LA

Conway alone submitted to a rich and growing enchantment. It was not so much any individual thing that attracted him as the gradual revelation of elegance, of modest and impeccable taste, of harmony so fragrant that it seemed to gratify the eye without arresting it.

— *James Hilton, "Lost Horizon," 1933*

IN MADAGASCAR'S CAPITAL, there are no traffic lights. Vintage Peugeots buck and sway to the jazz syncopation of *embouteillage*, the French word for traffic, straining up brick-red hills where for centuries Malagasy aristocrats entombed their ancestors. The Malagasy exhume their bodies every seven years, a ritual that sees death not as an ending, merely as a pause in the conversation.

For decades, Madagascar's president-for-life, Didier

Ratstiraka, had kept the island cut off from the rest of the world. Random messages filtered in, the song *Michele* by the Beatles, aerobics seen on satellite TV. But nobody had heard of Madonna and room service breakfast at the Saka-manga Hotel in Antananarivo still cost a dollar.

In 2009, when long-simmering discontent led to a coup d'etat, Madagascar's graceful improvisational music turned to cacophony. The desperately poor thronged the streets of the capital city of Antananarivo. Malnourished women no longer able to breast-feed their children begged money for powdered milk. Selling anything they had, often items as valueless as worn out socks, the poor overflowed the side-walks. Their misery was unmistakable, but it was the resig-nation on their faces that was most disturbing in a country known for its offbeat grace, the good manners of its people, a haunting music even in the midst of squalor.

"After the coup, there was a decline of any semblance of law and order," said Pier Larson, a professor of history at Johns Hopkins University. "Antananarivo had been a very orderly city, but it became a latrine. People selling things moved onto the streets. Motorcycles got up on the side-walks; one guy on a motorcycle hit me as I was walking by. It was like early 19th or 18th century London."

In the fall of 2013, when a presidential election went off without major incident, Madagascar stepped back from the brink of civil war. The election was hardly a panacea; neither candidate won a clear majority and a runoff is scheduled. Both candidates are proxies for former dictators, and if one prevails, some experts say, Madagascar could face another coup.

The best-case scenario is that, after a four-year descent into hell, Madagascar has a chance to right itself. It can't happen too soon. Madagascar has been struck by what is called "the resource curse." Mining and oil exploitation has already begun, including development of heavy oil fields using a technology similar to fracking. Industry sources report that Madagascar's burgeoning oil business is likely to be dwarfed by the development of natural gas. If industry estimates are correct, Madagascar's offshore gas reserves have been described as enough to power Western Europe for a decade. One industry commentator wrote: "If East Africa is hot, Madagascar is on fire."

Twenty-first-century globalization is landing with both feet—hard—on an island that has been described as "a world out of time."

LUXE, calme et volupté—luxury, tranquility and pleasure—is French symbolist poet Charles Baudelaire's description of Madagascar in his 1857 poem, *L'Invitation au Voyage*. Even now, well-traveled Africa hands get misty-eyed about Madagascar. There's something different about Madagascar, they say, and it's not only the island's unique plants and animals, even though these are scientifically valuable enough to have made Madagascar a priority for international conservation organizations for half a century.

When I first came to Madagascar in 2001, slash and burn farming had been decimating the country's forests for centuries. That was devastating enough, but nothing compared to the destruction caused by multinational mining and oil conglomerates, a ransacking of the world's fourth-largest island that was turbocharged by political instability.

Between 2001 and 2009, opening Madagascar to the world resulted in much-needed economic growth. But since 2009, the benefits of globalization have been overtaken by globalization's "social failures" as described by University of Massachusetts economist Arthur MacEwan: greater income inequality, environmental damage, and the decline of democratic control. Cute, furry lemurs may exist only on the world's fourth-largest island, but Madagascar's political troubles are endemic to the twenty-first century. Madagascar, once a snapshot of the distant past, now looks more like the dystopian future.

THANKS to its isolation and great size, Madagascar is the world's textbook example of convergent evolution: species that evolve similar traits by adapting to similar environments or ecological niches, even though they may be only distantly related or completely unrelated. Sometimes called "the eighth continent," Madagascar is a storehouse of evolution, not only famous for its lemurs, but for an estimated ten thousand endemic plants, many still uncatalogued by scientists. Six of the world's eight species of baobab tree exist only in Madagascar, along with twenty of the twenty-five species of *Pachypodium*, an enormous spiny plant like an elephant's trunk, six species of the giant spiny *Alluaudia*, and the list goes on. In 2011, the World Wildlife Fund reported that 600 new species of plants and animals had been discovered in Madagascar in the previous decade alone.

Apart from the French, who have a possessive relationship with all of their former colonies, but a particular fondness for Madagascar (*luxe, calme, volupté* and all that, including a rather repulsive predilection for sexual tourism) Americans tend to travel to Madagascar for the lemurs, but when they return, they usually come for the people. Humans came to the island no more than two thousand years ago, from Indonesia, Burma and Polynesia; these early arrivals were followed by East Africans, Arab slave traders, Indians and, in the 1600s, the French. From these diverse influences, Madagascar's culture evolved into something delicate yet universal. The central tenet is *fihavanana*: treat others as you would want to be treated. I had learned about *fihavanana* when I first traveled to Madagascar, but it was not until I returned that I understood how fragile it was, and how quickly culture, and an entire society, can be destroyed.

Fihavanana has been described as "the Malagasy expression of social intelligence" and "a basic principle of the collective life in Madagascar" incorporating friendship, filiation, tolerance, justice, harmony. The idea is so central to Malagasy life that it appears in the preamble to the country's constitution.

"The literal translation is difficult to capture," writes Wikipedia, "as the Malagasy culture applies the concept in unique ways. Its origin is *Havana*, meaning kin." A Peace Corps volunteer told me that the Malagasy people have a highly evolved and elaborate social structure but paid less attention to material culture, baskets and the like. I found most Malagasy similar to upper-class WASPs in their nuanced manners. Unlike Americans, they would never express disapproval or rejection when I committed a *faux pas*. Instead, an almost imperceptible twitch of a facial muscle indicating they were just so slightly wounded by my American idiocy would send me into paroxysms of guilt and make me want to do better.

When I arrived in Madagascar in 2001 on a fellowship to train environmental journalists, I was shocked by the country's poverty. After a few days on Île aux Nattes and Île Sainte-Marie, where the semi-mythical pirate state of

Libertaria once existed (or perhaps not) I realized that Madagascar had always lived in my mind—if only in negative space. Even as a kid, I'd sensed there was something inhuman in America's unforgiving hustle. In Madagascar, money was not the measure of all things; in fact, it barely seemed to exist. I heard the Malagasy proverb "Ny Fihavanana no talohan'ny vola," which, loosely translated, means "the relationship is more important than the money."

In Madagascar, colors looked brighter, and the rhythm of life felt fluid. Culture and nature were oddly congruent: The mouse lemur in a nest of branches and the watchman strumming a stringed instrument and singing softly, both tuned to the same refrain under a sky of falling stars. Here, in this country of eroding elegance and sweeping landscape, the parallel world of my imagination turned out to be real.

That Madagascar was real, but like Shangri-La, illusory. Earlier waves of globalization had doomed the elephant birds, ten feet tall and eight hundred pounds, sloth lemurs the size of grizzly bears, and pygmy hippos, all driven to extinction.

Humanity itself is just as fragile, if one defines the word as the quality of being humane. Contemporary scholars have criticized the Shangri-La of the 1933 novel "Lost Horizon" as Orientalism, the fetishization of the Exotic that is the flip side of colonial oppression. But the book's dominant theme is the yearning to preserve a sense of humanity in the wake of World War I, even as World War II gathered outside the confines of James Hilton's mythical lamasery.

Like "Lost Horizon," Madagascar is a reminder of how quickly not only nature, but a civilization, can be destroyed. Indeed, one might even think the two are related.

THE QUEEN'S Palace looms in ruined splendor atop what was once the highest of the twelve hills surrounding Antananarivo. Built for Queen Ranavalona I between 1839 and 1841, the palace and its surrounding structures burned in 1995, days before they were to be inscribed in the list of UNESCO World Heritage sites. The fire was believed to be arson by coastal people revolting against the dominance of the high plateau's Merina aristocrats. But the palace resisted: The building's walls, originally constructed of wood, had been encased in stone by a Scottish mason. Like Miss Havisham's decaying mansion, the shell survived, a still point in Madagascar's tumultuous history.

Scholars say that Madagascar has been dominated by a feudal aristocracy, families descended from the Indonesians who made their way to the island across fifteen hundred miles of ocean. Yet for more than thirty-five years, a canny politician named Didier Ratsiraka, who came not from the high plateau, but from the coast, was the country's president-for-life. Ratsiraka rose to power as a socialist, but when aid dried up from communist countries after the fall of the Berlin Wall, he turned toward the West. In reality, Madagascar had always retained ties with France, a country notoriously reluctant to relinquish interests in its former colonies.

During the Ratsiraka years, Madagascar remained largely isolated from the rest of the world, not unlike North Korea, one of Ratsiraka's major supporters. "A World Out of Time" was the title guitarists Henry Kaiser and David Lindley gave to their recordings of master Malagasy musicians. Their landmark 1991 CD featured musicians playing instruments unique to Madagascar, sonic equivalents of the island's rare lemurs and chameleons: the delicate *sodina* flute and the *valiha*, a tube zither made of local bamboo. If there was a star, it was D'Gary, who translated the music of Madagascar's stringed instruments to guitar. In those days, D'Gary's music was one of the few examples of a cultural exchange with the West.

In reality, Madagascar had never been completely isolated. in the 1600s, the island's French governor put a Francophone stamp on the island's feudal system. The Arab slave trade of the 1700s left its mark. In the 1800s, after the British ended the trade in the Indian Ocean, Merina aristocrats established an internal slave economy to build their empire.

In 2001, another watershed event changed the island: Antananarivo's mayor, self-made millionaire Marc Ravalomanana, ran for president. Turning to the U.S. rather than France, he hired crack political operatives recommended by Kurt Schmoke, the first African-American mayor of Baltimore, who had become a friend and mentor during Ravalomanana's business trips to the U.S. After an 11-month standoff over election results, the upstart Ravalomanana became Madagascar's president.

Madagascar had already started to embrace a twenty-first-century economy. Construction had begun on the country's first major industrial development, an $800 million mine controlled by international mining giant Rio Tinto Zinc that could produce ten percent of the world's titanium dioxide. The project included a major shipping port near Fort Dauphin on Madagascar's southeast coast.

Madagascar was waking from centuries of reverie. After the mine opened, the surf still broke over old shipwrecks, but the sleepy colonial city of Fort Dauphin had been transformed into a boomtown. Prostitution and nightclubs flourished, along with sexually transmitted diseases, although, for reasons that baffle researchers, AIDS did not become prevalent. But few of the company's promises of jobs, health care and education for local communities materialized.

The country's new president said all the right things. Neoliberal capitalism was a natural fit for this bootstrap millionaire and he quickly won support from the World Bank, essential for managing the country's perennial debt. Partnering with advisers at Harvard University, Ravalomanana launched an economic growth initiative that included establishing incentives for foreign investment, privatization of state industries—and birth control. At the 2003 Durban World Parks Congress, he endeared himself to foreign donors by declaring economic growth and environmental protection inseparable, pledging to protect ten percent of the country's land in five years.

Ravalomanana followed through on many of his promises. His administration established health care facilities and primary schools, set aside large tracts of land for conservation, and improved Madagascar's stunningly decrepit road network. It didn't hurt that Ravalomanana was fluent in English, which he had learned as a student in Denmark, and stunningly handsome.

Ravalomanana won decisive re-election in 2006. His second-term platform, the Madagascar Action Plan, which set targets for additional development, was lauded as state of the art. By 2008, Madagascar's economy was booming with 6.3 percent growth. Critics in Madagascar's business community complained that the figures were inflated, but the change was undeniable. Late-model Toyotas appeared on the newly paved streets of Antananarivo, along with those bellwethers of modernity: advertising billboards.

Madagascar's future looked promising, as did Ravalomanana's. The country's incipient mining boom was predicted to create as many as 100,000 jobs. The French oil company Total was backing tar sands development in the country's southwest, and an enormous cadmium and nickel mine run by Canadian company Sherritt International promised to become a major employer. The Sherritt mine would have an impact on rare and endemic species - one biologist described running ahead of a bulldozer digging out plants that were new to science - by industry standards the company was attempting to show concern both for the environment and the need to create jobs for Malagasy workers.

Outside the well-paved capital, discontent was escalating. Only a small percentage of Malagasy people were benefiting from the boom times. Madagascar's standard of living had been in decline long before Ravalomanana's presidency. The population had grown exponentially, but slash and burn farming left vast tracts of land depleted after as little as seven years. In the 1960s, Madagascar had been a net exporter of agricultural products. Now the country imported most of its food.

Ravalomanana let the exchange rate for Malagasy currency float, which aided growth but caused inflation to escalate. The cost of living was rising dramatically, not just in Madagascar, but worldwide. The Malagasy Ariary's precipitous drop in comparison with the Euro deepened the hardships. As late as 2005, eighty-five percent of Madagascar's people were living on less than $2 a day. Much of Madagascar remained untouched by modernity. Child labor was commonplace, with one-fifth of those between the ages of five and fourteen working, often in dangerous industries such as mining or stone cutting.

By 2008, inflation had reached 27 percent. To make it worse, Ravalomanana seemed to be changing. "Marc" as he urged supporters to call him, was a genuine Horatio Alger. Starting at the age of five, the Protestant choirboy walked four kilometers to school, often leaving early to sell water-cress to train passengers. He subsidized his secondary school studies by selling yogurt in individual serving pots to local villagers and students, an enterprise that grew into Madagascar's largest food conglomerate.

Now that he was most powerful man in the country, Ravalomanana seemed unable to temper his ambition. He used his presidency to benefit his companies and he made a sweetheart deal to lease nearly half of Madagascar's arable land to the South Korean agricultural firm Daewoo for corn and palm oil plantations. In a country where more than half the population consists of small farmers, this galvanized the opposition, despite the promise of thousands of jobs.

The Daewoo deal was uncommon only in its size and scope. While people in Madagascar are quick to distinguish themselves from the rest of Africa, Ravalomanana was replaying a familiar post-colonial scenario: an autocratic leader cutting deals that have more than a whiff of neocolo-nialism. Most recently, the sought-after commodity has been land. Since 2000, there had been nearly one thousand deals to lease agricultural land in Kenya, Ethiopia, Sudan, and the Democratic Republic of Congo.

As the furor over the Daewoo deal intensified, Ravalo-manana committed the politically tone deaf sin of using international funds to purchase a second multimillion-dollar presidential jet. When he attempted to cut the mili-tary budget, street demonstrations broke out in Antana-narivo. Ravalomanana's successor as the capital's mayor, a thirty-five-year-old former disc jockey and TV station owner named Andry Rajoelina, whose rabble-rousing stations had been shut down by an increasingly authori-tarian Ravolamanana, became the figurehead for an insur-gency backed by military leaders. It was widely believed that the military, many members of which had ties to Ratsiraka, were backed by powerful French interests, including the oil company Total. But the tiny handful of foreign reporters in Madagascar who might have broken the story without fear of reprisal never found a paper trail.

By then, Ravalomanana had lost the support of the aristocratic families of the Haut Plateau. The Merina high caste had never considered Ravalomanana one of their own; now the word *hova*, the caste of commoners who engage in business and whose family tombs lie outside the walls of high-caste enclaves, was regularly appended to the president's name.

"It's embarrassing to see him on TV," a prominent businesswoman in the capital complained. "He can't even speak French properly."

The increasingly autocratic Ravalomanana had engineered his own downfall, and he brought Madagascar down with him. One of the signs that power had gone to Ravalomanana's head may seem trivial, but in terms of day-to-day life, it was unmistakable. As mayor, Ravalomanana had spruced up Antananarivo, planting flowers in parks and along road medians, improving trash collection and installing streetlights to combat crime. As president, he went further, ordering owners of the city's 1960s-vintage Peugeot taxis to paint their vehicles a uniform dull yellow instead of the city's distinctive candy colors of pink, blue and green.

The swinging jazz of the daily *embouteillage* slowed to a dirge.

IN MARCH 2009, after street demonstrations became increasingly violent and tensions continued to escalate, military leaders reportedly persuaded Ravalomanana to resign. Andry Rajoelina, too young to run for president under Madagascar's constitution, took nominal control of the government in what news agencies called a coup d'etat. The transfer of power was relatively low-key, as coups go: Fewer than 100 people died in the street demonstrations culminating in Ravalomanana's ouster. Human rights organizations either ignored the events in Madagascar, or gave the situation minimal attention. In the U.S., there was virtually no news coverage.

"Madagascar's paradoxical problem is that its culture is essentially nonviolent," remarked Kevin Doyle, an American who has spent much of his career directing aid and development projects in conflict zones throughout sub-Saharan Africa. Without the grisly narratives that reinforce stereotypes of Africa, Doyle said, the Western world ignores countries like Madagascar.

Over the next four years, Madagascar descended into a state of misery beyond the grasp of most Westerners. Under Rajoelina's so-called transitional government, Madagascar's GDP growth fell from 7 percent in 2008 to *minus* 3.7 percent. By 2013, the World Bank estimated that 92 percent of the population was living on less than $2 a day. Acute child malnutrition increased by fifty percent. An estimated six hundred thousand children had to leave school because their families could not pay tuition fees.

With poverty, hunger and desperation on the rise, *fihavanana* became a luxury few could afford. Theft and violent crime increased. Madagascar's culture was eroding, both its tradition and its nascent progress.

"These developments put the welfare of future generations at risk," concluded a World Bank report. "At this point, Madagascar will not reach most of the UN Millennium Development Goals (MDG) by 2015, even the ones which in 2007 were deemed potentially achievable (e.g., reducing child mortality, increasing enrollment in primary education, and eradicating extreme poverty)."

To make matters worse, in a move intended to put pressure on Rajoelina to resolve Madagascar's political crisis, the U.S. and other donors cut off all but humanitarian aid. Foreign aid totaling roughly $400 million had accounted for nearly half the government's budget and three-quarters of public spending.

Madagascar's textile industry had been thriving, partly because of the African Growth and Opportunity Act, which enables African governments to access the U.S. market without paying duty if they show a commitment to democracy. When the Obama administration suspended the agreement, 50,000 workers in factories that made clothes for the U.S. market lost their jobs.

News coverage, such as it was, fixated on high-level negotiations among the current and former heads of state: Rajoelina, Ravalomanana, former President Albert Zafy and the shadowy *eminence grise* of Madagascar politics, longtime head of state Didier Ratsiraka. The poverty, misery, and death of Madagascar's people received little attention. The few articles that appeared in the U.S. were investigations of corrupt military leaders profiting from illegal logging of rosewood trees from national parks and conservation areas. While the logging destroyed habitat for the silky Sifaka lemur, one of the world's most endangered species, this was a bellwether for even greater losses tied to Ravalomanana's fall.

Since the 1800s, the destruction of forests for slash and burn agriculture had left Madagascar with less than five percent of its original landscape. A longtime resident says she charted the dissolution of Madagascar's civil society by the billowing smoke on the road from the capital to her home. From 2004 to 2008, when Ravalomanana was in office, the sky was clear. By 2010, the horizon was dense with yellow smoke from burning trees. "It was horrific," she said.

Richard Marcus, who heads the Global Studies Institute at California State University at Long Beach recently wrote a book on Madagascar. He believes the country's crisis was prolonged by a series of missteps by Western nations and the donor community's bureaucratic self-interest.

"In 2009 suddenly donors were talking about reputational risk," Marcus said. "The World Bank had invested a significant amount in Madagascar since 2002 and they thought: 'Are we going to lose face here?' "

As successive rounds of negotiations failed, Madagascar's suffering deepened; a meanness of spirit crept in, and the culture of mild complaint that had been ubiquitous during the Ratsiraka years turned to hopelessness and anger.

"The four heads of state approach showed a lack of knowledge about Madagascar," Marcus said. "The assumption that the four of them represented Malagasy society was just incorrect. The talks left all the other players out of the process, including 150 political parties and organizations that were promoting a stronger civil society."

He believes that the underlying premise of the talks—that Madagascar remained, at bottom, a feudal aristocracy—was outdated. "It used to be essential to woo the big Merina families in the capital," he said. "But Ravalomanana is not from that caste. Rajoelina is also not from that caste. The idea that there is an important business class that is nouveau riche came about in the 1990s and was even more prevalent in the early 2000s. The old families are important, but not as important."

What remains from Madagascar's feudalism is a tale of rivalry and revenge straight outta Shakespeare: Ratsiraka, from his comfortable exile in France, threw his support behind Rajoelina, reportedly still furious over his defeat by Ravalomanana. By normal standards, Ratsiraka was a war criminal. Substantial documentation existed that his guard had opened fire on demonstrators in 1991. In 2003, he was convicted of stealing from Madagascar's central bank. These are only the offenses that reached public view. Ratsiraka had come to power after the assassination of Madagascar's only political hero, Richard Ratsimandrava. Shot under mysterious circumstances only six days after assuming the presidency in 1975, Ratsimandrava wanted to restore Madagascar's tradition of village democracy. He is still called the Malagasy John F. Kennedy, and rumors still circulate that Ratsiraka was involved in his assassination.

Ratsiraka consolidated his power not only by punishing his enemies, but by incrementally restructuring Madagascar's laws and stacking the courts, as Siaka Stevens did in Sierra Leone, and, some might argue, Republicans have done in the United States. After winning election as an anti-corruption crusader, Ravalomanana was accused of using his presidency to establish monopolies for his companies, as well as avoiding taxes. But like Ratsiraka, he was careful to act within the law, simply changing laws and regulations when it suited him. Rajoelina, by taking power in a coup, stepped outside the law, taking the process to its logical conclusion.

There were no heroes at the peace talks. Ravalomanana had been sentenced to life imprisonment for ordering his guard to open fire on demonstrators, killing thirty of them. The international community considered the trial politically motivated—Ravalomanana himself called it "a mock trial"—but in the end, Ravalomanana agreed not to run for president. Instead, his wife Lalao would be a candidate. Neither Ratsiraka nor Ravalomanana ever acknowledged wrongdoing.

Eventually all of the past players—including Lalao Ravalomanana—were barred from running for president. The election took place without major incident on Oct. 25, 2013.

AFTER THE VOTES WERE COUNTED, political scientist Marcus sounded not quite euphoric, but relieved. "It isn't democracy, but it's a step," he said. "You have a surprising moment right now that no one would have fully anticipated. The two parties tired themselves out and were edged out of the process. Personally, I feel they should disappear from the planet."

Inside Madagascar, people were less sanguine, invoking the phrase *plus ça change, plus c'est la même chose* (the more it changes, the more it remains the same). The two leading candidates had ties to Ravalomanana and Rajoelina. On the campaign trail, front-runner Jean-Louis Robinson, a doctor who served as minister of health in Ravalomanana's administration, had repeatedly promised to appoint Ravalomanana's wife Lalao as prime minister.

Robinson won 21 percent of the votes, a comfortable lead in a field of more than 100 candidates, but under Malagasy law, short of the 50 percent needed to avoid a runoff election, which will be held Dec. 20. In the event of an upset, there is talk that his opponent, Hery Rajaonarimampianina, will name coup leader Rajoelina as prime minister.

"It was a mistake by the international community to allow people like who took part in the transition government—who were never elected and were tied to coup leaders—to run for president," said a prominent Malagasy business leader. "It's led by France. They just want an election and to get back to business. They don't care how it happens."

In the end, it was Rajaonarimampianina who won the Dec. 20 runoff election. He did not appoint Andry Rajoelina, the former coup leader and front man for the generals, to a post in government. The country tottered back into relative stability, but nothing was the same. Street crime in Antananarivo soared. A different mood was in the streets. They smelled like fear.

But once again the magic world "election" restored Western aid: The World Bank budget for Madagascar in 2013 was $167 million.

Perhaps the new government could be held accountable. A semblance of democracy might appear in a remote island ruled by all-powerful aristocrats who disinterred their ancestors every seven years to be possessed by their spirits. People who worshipped the past.

IN 2006, at the behest of then-President Ravalomanana, workers restored the ruins of the Queen's Palace. By 2008, the interior had been rebuilt, using cement to withstand the ravages of time and political unrest. The partially restored structure was opened to the public, but closed soon afterward so work could resume.

It never did. After the *coup d'etat*, work on the palace

halted. Left alone on its hill, Queen Ranavalona's palace watched over the city.

It is worth noting that Queen Ranavalona was no mere figurehead. Ruling from 1828 until her death in 1861, she resisted foreign exploitation of the island's resources, raised a standing army of 20,000, and expanded her empire, often using forced labor. She also preached, unsuccessfully, against the environmentally destructive practice of slash and burn farming.

Until recently, historians regarded her as a tyrant, and some called her insane. More recently, they have recast her as a leader protecting her people from European colonial domination. In the last election, Madagascar's female candidates, free of ties to the country's tainted leadership, evoked a thin thread of hope, even among the capital's most cynical observers. Saraha Rabearisoa, an ecologist, was considered the most credible candidate. As the founder of the country's green party, Rabearisoa heads a grass-roots organization strong enough to make it a contender in upcoming parliamentary elections. The second largest vote-getter among the women, Brigitte Rabemanantsoa, is a medical doctor, and a former president of the Association of Madagascar's Female Mayors. A third candidate, Roseline Emma Rasolovoahangy, was barred from running because she had not spent enough time in the country. But Rasolovoahangy is unlikely to give up. A geophysicist and energy entrepreneur with a Ph.D. from Stanford, she is a fierce competitor who once captained Madagascar's women's national basketball team.

Madagascar's graceful society developed over thousands of years, but it has taken less than a decade to put it on life support. The country's rapid fall after a decade of peace and economic growth is a reminder of the sudden turns history can take. It begins with perfectly legal changes to an obscure rule, or perhaps a series of politically motivated court appointments — Didier Ratsiraka's alterations to Madagascar's constitution or the resolution rammed through the U.S. Congress that gave a Republican majority the absolute right to shut down government. Maryland representative Chris Van Hollen, a mainstream Democrat, suggested exactly this in a heated exchange with the Republican leadership.

"Why were the rules rigged to keep the government shut down?" asks Van Hollen.

"The gentleman will suspend," interrupts Jason Chaffetz, the Utah Republican presiding on behalf of majority leader John Boehner.

"*Democracy* has been suspended," Van Hollen retorted.

This was in 2013, three years before the election of Donald J. Trump.

LARSON, who has spent more time in Madagascar than most Westerners, sees the country's problems not as relics of feudalism or a dark continent, but as emblematic of a postmodern globalized world. While cultures remain distinct, although less so than before, the forces pushing on them are global.

"Obviously, Madagascar has history of *coup d'etats*, or popular uprisings," Larson said. "A lot of changes haven't been done according to the ballot box. So it's not surprising that people who have power and influence attempt to exercise it. But the difficulty with bringing new people into leadership positions and the fact that the military eats a lot of the national budget, these are problems not unique to Madagascar."

If globalization results in greater income inequality,

environmental damage, and the decline of democratic control, what can Madagascar tell us about the rest of the world, I asked Larson.

"Things can change very quickly," he said. "Who would have predicted that Ethiopia would become one of the fastest-growing economies in the world? This may be slightly dramatic, but what if the U.S. comes to a complete political impasse, and there's no way out? What happens when you have a population completely disgusted with all the political figures? That's a population ripe to support a *coup d'etat*.

"I'm an historian," Larson continued. "I teach about the distant past. You see the rise and fall of states. They last two years, or three. None of them last a thousand years."

THERE IS ONLY one valley of Blue Moon, and those who expect to find another are asking too much of nature.

—James Hilton *Lost Horizon* 1933

SIX

JE SUIS COMMANDO

I'm writing this to pay a debt. In 2009, I taught at an American university in Dakar, Senegal. My students were not Americans; they were Africans, rich kids from all over the continent, but mostly West Africa: Nigeria, Mali, Guinea-Bissau, The Gambia, and, of course, Senegal itself, where the first president was a poet, Leopold Senghor, and the people are known for their devotion to the arts and their arrogance, which, as Africans from neighboring countries point out, is so much like the French.

When you live in Dakar, you notice two things right away. Despite a rash of new construction along the Corniche, the city's seafront promenade, horse-drawn carts still carry fruits and vegetables, cooking oil, and bolts of fabric to shops. The clip clop of horses' hooves is the first thing you hear in the morning. It is quite romantic, even though you are already sweating because the power is out and your air conditioner is not running.

The second thing you notice are the *talibés*. A block inland from the mansions built by Nigerian oil wealth and the drug trade, you will encounter feral boys who haunt the streets dressed in rags. They are, officially, students of the Koran. In reality, they are slaves. Some are as young as five. There are 30,000 of them in the Dakar region alone, three percent of the population in a city of slightly more than one million, many living in overcrowded shacks where they sleep piled on each other like puppies.

Talibé translates to "student" or "seeker" and in Senegal, the word is used for children in Koranic schools called darras. Until the late 1970s, *talibés* attended these schools in their home villages. But when Senegal's agricultural economy collapsed in the late 1970s, a victim of drought, the Koranic teachers, and their students, migrated to Senegal's cities.

The traditional system devolved into slavery. In modern-day Dakar, when *talibés* fail to make the quota their teachers set for them - roughly an average day's wage for an adult - they are beaten with chains, strips of tires, or wet ropes. If they run away, the punishment can be worse. Human rights activists report that some *darras* have punishment rooms, which often contain a pole with a chain. Chained to the pole, runaways are forced to sit on their bound wrists and ankles. One Senegalese activist called it torture.

"After only an hour you are suffering, and in some *darras* I know, they have to stay there for a whole day," he said. "They do it so that it hurts and so the boy won't run away anymore."

"When I think of it slavery comes to mind," he added.

There are an estimated fifty thousand *talibés* in Senegal, and their numbers are increasing as human traffickers bring boys in from neighboring countries, according to Corinne Dufka, Associate Director at Human Rights Watch. Just as my students came to Dakar to prepare for joining West Africa's one percent, poor children are sent to the region's largest city to take their places in society. *Talibés* trafficked from neighboring countries now make up one-third to half of Dakar's child beggars, according to Anti-Slavery International. The enslavement of *talibés* is fueled by poverty, high numbers of children in families — and deeply held traditions that value humility and learning the Koran, according to Dufka.

"I believe the *talibés* are a blind spot in Senegal," Dufka said. "People don't see the abuse anymore, because it's so common. You become desensitized because it's so difficult to take in.

"It takes leadership to say, 'This is is abuse and it's happening right before our eyes.' Can you imagine in the United States, seeing children on the streets during school hours begging, with no shoes, and some of them clearly ill? I believe the sight of these kids, so many of them over the years, has numbed the authorities who are mandated to protect these children."

AS I WENT about my life in Dakar, rushing to work, buying food at the roadside kiosks, I began to ignore the *talibés*, too. Dirty, unsocialized, gut-wrenchingly sad, occasionally threatening, there were simply too many of them. I wrote the situation off as hopeless, until a colleague introduced me to Yaya Sidibé.

Sidibé is a product of the *talibé* system before it went bad. A tall, fortyish man with greyhound energy, Sidibé arrives at one of Dakar's quasi-French cafes carrying a heavily laden Targus daypack. He places it carefully on the floor, explaining that it contains medicines, medicaments, to treat the wounds and skin diseases that *talibés* suffer from abuse and unsanitary conditions.

Je suis commando, he said, with a weary grin..

Sidibé's own Koranic education started when he was five. By the age of seven, he was putting in ten-hour days attending both state-run schools and Koranic school. He worked on a farm on weekends, bringing in the harvests that would feed the Koranic school's students. He jokes that he never had weekends, so he doesn't miss them; it's only his wife who wishes he was home more often.

Sidibé thrived as a *talibé* in his home village. But while attending vocational school in St. Louis, one of Senegal's larger cities, he ran out of money and found himself living on the streets. He was taken in by a home for boys run by a Catholic social services organization, where one of the priests suggested he write a letter on behalf of a prisoner in Mexico.

"Four months later the priest asked, 'Do you remember I gave you a notice about a Mexican?' Your letter contributed to his release," Sidibé recalled.

The Muslim teenager became a convert; not to Christianity but to the cause of human rights. At fourteen, Amnesty International hired Sidibé to teach high school students about human rights. He continued working for Amnesty while studying at the University of Dakar, and in 1997, he went to his superiors with a not-so-modest proposal: remove all *talibés* from Koranic schools.

All of them? his boss asked.

Absolutement, Sidibé replied without hesitating.

Too ambitious, they said.

By 2004, Sidibé was ready to create his own organization, but Senegal was not ready for him. Sidibé says that he filed all the necessary paperwork with the police and prefecture...and waited. Two years later, when the authorities told him they had lost his documents, he started the process again. This time, he was asked for a bribe, which he refused to pay.

Nobody was eager to help him take on the enormous power of Senegal's Muslim brotherhoods, whose lower-echelon teachers ran the *darras*. The *marabouts* were simply too well-connected.

A combination of K Street lobbyists, traditional healers, and con artists, Senegal's marabouts are immensely powerful, and, despite the country's modern appearance, they have lost none of their clout. In the 2007 novel *Allah is Not Obliged* by the great Cote d'Ivoirean writer Amadou Kourouma, a naughty kid named Birahima, tells a picaresque tale of how he was kidnapped to become a child soldier through the machinations of marabouts: Balla, the sorcerer and master huntsman who crippled Birahima's mother with traditional medicine; the money-multiplier Yacouba, and Sekou, "a vicious crook" who could pull a "white chicken clucking out of the sleeve of his bou bou."

Allah is Not Obliged is the archetypal tale of an orphan boy tricked by con men and criminals, a West African version of *Oliver Twist*, *Candide*, and *Huckleberry Finn*. But the power of the marabouts is no joke; if anything, it is frightening. In Senegal's hierarchical culture, these keepers of the Koran's secrets are so respected that an unknown *marabout* can arrive in a village, and simply by virtue of his authority, parents will entrust their children to his care. As Sidibé said: "In Africa, kids respect adults and one kid is everyone's kid."

The brotherhoods' power was visible in sharp relief after eight young *talibés* burned to death in a fire at the makeshift shack that served as their *darra* in Dakar in 2013.

After the fire, Senegal's new president Mackey Sall, who had been elected as a reformer, promised to end the exploitation of the *talibés*. Neighbors, local officials and activists identified four schools where dangerous conditions existed. One was closed and its students returned to their families.

But after the Muslim brotherhoods forced a meeting with President Sall, authorities dropped plans to close schools and prosecute abusive marabouts, according to a 2015 report by Human Rights Watch. A 2005 law that criminalizes forced begging has not been enforced and proposed legislation that would bring the *darras* under state control, supported by a wide range of civil society and human rights activists, has stalled out, largely because of the political clout of the Muslim brotherhoods.

Of the country's four brotherhoods, the most powerful is the Mouride, which counts singer Youssou N'Dour among its members. Founded in the early twentieth century by Sufi mystic Amadou Bamba, the sect enshrines nonviolence and hard work. Members of the sect, who number in the millions, function as a tightly knit mutual aid society; for example, the men selling knockoff hats, umbrellas, and knockoff Prada purses in Manhattan are part of a highly organized Mouride business.

Youssou N'Dour has argued that the precepts of Mouridism are a counterweight to the post-9/11 version of Islam, and the sect's mystical bent has made it unpopular among hardline Islamic fundamentalists.

"In the West, you read all about terrorism," N'Dour told a BBC reporter. "We're all lumped together. But those of us who understand that it's a religion of peace, love, and sharing mustn't give up."

While child beggars are more ubiquitous than ever,

N'Dour is not being disingenuous: progressive Mouride leaders are making efforts to modernize Koranic schools. A descendant of the Mouride brotherhood's founder, Sokhna Mama Issa Mbaké, supports thirteen model *darras*, where boys — and girls — learn French, Arabic, science and computer literacy.

ONLY A FEW CHILDREN come from families that can afford the tuition at high-powered private schools. According to a Senegalese government study, more than half of the Koranic schools in the Dakar region provide no education other than learning the Koran. In many so-called *darras*, human rights activists say, children receive an hour or two of rote memorization or no education at all. The guiding principle is not religion; it is profit: it is not uncommon for unethical marabouts to make $100,000 a year off the backs of child slaves.

One Senegalese activist — not Sidibé — told Human Rights Watch that when he meets a *talibé*, the first thing he does is look at his back for the marks of a beating. He talked about a ten-year-old boy who had been beaten with a horse-whip. The boy explained what he did to survive.

"You just think about your home," he said.

This activist echoed the words of many who are familiar with the *talibés*, saying that the best solution is for the boys to be returned to their families. But even that solution is not simple. The countryside is poor, and the *talibé* tradition deeply embedded in Senegalese society. In fact, marabouts often send their own children out begging. As they get older, the marabouts put them in charge of the other boys, and they are inculcated into the culture of abuse.

"They say the kids are mentally sick," Sidibé says. "No,

it's the people dressed like me," - he grabs the lapels of his jacket - "who abuse them. They are the ones who are sick."

Even though the *talibé* system has been perverted almost beyond recognition, the authority of marabouts is so entrenched that unless there is strong leadership on the issue — and the funding to improve conditions in the *darras* — even more boys will be subjected to the hellish conditions of Senegal's modern-day slave pens. Even Sidibé, a fire-brand in nearly every other respect, is reluctant to criticize the marabouts, saying that they are merely part of a system, and it is the system that needs to change.

"I didn't come in judgment. I came with bleach," Sidibé says, adding, with the Senegalese version of a Gallic shrug, "I am a *talibé*."

A shadow crosses his face. In the silence that follows, it is clear that Sidibé was about to say that current-day *talibés* are not truly talibés. But he stopped himself, because times have changed. The abused feral boys on Dakar's streets are the real *talibés* now.

SEVEN

SULEIMAN'S TRAVELS

"Honey, I've been thinking we should hyphenate. You know, Zakin-Suleiman. Or Suleiman-Zakin."

"We can talk about that later," he mutters.

We are halfway down the jetway, waiting to find out whether we can get back on our flight to San Francisco. A flight attendant's voice had come over the loudspeaker, asking my husband and another guy with a Muslim name to get off the Delta flight scheduled to depart from JFK. It is the 10th anniversary of 9/11.

When I booked our tickets, I didn't make the connection. What can I say? I spent most of my career as an environmental writer. Hurricane Katrina looms larger for me than 9/11 in "American exceptionalism is dead" symbolism. An alternative theory was proposed by my then-therapist, who believed that people with intrusive mothers tend to zone out on large public events they can't control.

Whatever. All I know is that what happened to us over the next few hours was very different from the experience of Shoshana Hebshi, the half-Arab, half-Jewish housewife strip searched by Homeland Security officers on that same day. Our experience made me think that America was getting it right when it came to security. What roils me is average Americans' ignorance of their own country's foreign policy.

I wasn't quite so Zen when I heard my husband's name over the PA system; I shot out of my seat even faster than my beleaguered significant other. My husband is from Lamu Island, off the Kenyan coast, one of those hippie highway destinations, like Ibiza, frequented by ex-models, minor royalty and various Rolling Stones. I am from the Upper East Side of Manhattan. I do most things faster.

"SORRY! COMMON MUSLIM NAME," I explained to the blond, tired-looking man in our row as I stepped over him.

"I'm Finnish," he said, waving his hand, as if to say, we Scandinavians are too evolved for all your crazy American paranoia.

Needless to say, I had more bags than my husband, so he went on ahead while I wrestled with my laptop, shoulder bag and overstuffed carry-on. When I reached the waiting area near gate 26, I was relieved to see him seated across from a very large man with curly brown hair. At least they hadn't whisked him into an interrogation room. The man, who wore a name tag that identified him as an immigration official, gestured that it was OK for me to sit down.

"Have you been out of the country recently?" he asked my husband.

"Yes."

"When did you leave?"

I watched my husband struggle. It was a real DSK moment. Not because my husband wanted to lie, but because exact dates and times aren't as important in Africa as they are here, except among the highly educated. Half the Africans I've met don't know how old they are, much less the exact date they traveled somewhere.

"Early May," I said. "He went back to take care of his kids."

The rest of it pretty much went like that. The immigration guy asked questions. Sometimes one of us answered, sometimes the other. I found a way of inserting the fact that I was Jewish and originally from New York into the conversation. I also mentioned that I was a reporter. Not exactly marriage material for a devout Muslim, much less a card-carrying Islamic extremist.

All the agent wanted to know was whether my husband had been to Somalia recently or donated money to Somali organizations. My husband got a little huffy, which sent me into a panic. You had to know the back story to understand his reaction. The coastal region of Kenya, where my husband's family has lived for about eight hundred years, is next door to Somalia. Kenyans tend to consider Somalis ratfuck crazy, not to mention heavily armed. Somali bandits have been coming over the border and causing various kinds of mayhem since the 1960s, when a commentator, no doubt a devoted listener of radio serials, coined the term "The Shifta Menace." (Shifta is the word used in most of East Africa for bandit or rebel.) Somali bandits are blamed for any crime that hasn't been solved yet, from poaching to the recent kidnapping of a British tourist.

The U.S. government's attention to Somalia as a potential terrorist threat struck me as well placed. Few Americans even know that in late 2006, the United States supported Ethiopia's invasion of Somalia. The U.S. supported the Ethiopian invasion because of a perceived rightward tilt of the Islamic Courts Union, which ruled the country at the time. The courts had provided Somalia's first stable government in sixteen years. The courts had been relatively moderate, and some observers contend that U.S. pressure was partly to blame for the regime's alliances with Islamic fundamentalists.

I'm dubious about that contention. But I agree with Aidan Hartley, a Kenyan-born journalist who has probably covered Somalia longer and better than any Western journalist. Hartley has warned of an anti-U.S. backlash. In Somalia, Hartley wrote, the U.S. may be "helping to transform a backwater tribal conflict into what could turn out to be the worst Islamist insurgency in the world after Iraq and Afghanistan."

So far, Hartley's words have proved to be prescient. With the ouster of the Islamic Courts, Somalia became Mad Max land again, with key regions controlled by Al Shabaab, a fundamentalist group that announced in February it had aligned itself with al-Qaida. Recently, Al Shabaab suspended aid programs organized by the U.N. and others, exacerbating the flood of refugees into Kenya.

At the same time, I understand why the U.S. was alarmed by the Islamic Courts, which offered refuge to terrorists. The invasion by Ethiopia, Somalia's historical rival, gave U.S. bombers cover to go after Fazul Abdullah Mohammed, the al-Qaida operative called the "mastermind" behind the attacks on the U.S. embassies in Nairobi and Dar es Salaam in 1998 and an Israeli-owned hotel in Mombasa, on the Kenyan coast, in 2002. The U.S. bombers fumbled, according to news reports, succeeding in killing approximately seventy sheep and pissing off a few nomads. But Fazul was killed in June, chalking up another hit for the Obama administration's surprisingly steroidal counterterrorism effort. (If only the president could be so macho when he deals with Republicans, I remember thinking.)

After I met my husband at a writers conference on Lamu, I realized that the notorious Fazul had not only spent time on the archipelago, but he had also married a local girl, a fifteen-year-old student at a madrassa where he taught under a pseudonym. I went back to the island, partly to see if my nascent romance was anything more than a holiday fling, and partly because I thought I should try to cover the story. I was tired of editors telling me that I was a good writer but the environment didn't sell. So I tried to convince myself that I could write a story about Fazul, even though I considered both radical Islamists and George W. Bush delusional, testosterone-crazed morons who should be paying attention to their respective economies instead of engaging in pointless wars. I was more interested in Fazul's wife, who had been picked up by Kenyan police, than Fazul himself.

I did a week or two of cursory reporting before heading up to the Laikipia Plateau to research an environmental story. I discovered that the woman detained by Kenyan authorities was actually Fazul's first wife, not the local girl he had married, who had since divorced him. I also discovered that the Muslim women in Kenya were not necessarily eager to be liberated or to talk to the American media, even if one played the sisterhood card. Their sisters wore veils.

In the end, I got a personal rejection letter from David Remnick at the *New Yorker*, calling my story idea "novel" but explaining he used staff writers for stories like mine. I wanted to respond that people who hung around Manhattan and Brooklyn and sucked up to *New Yorker* editors were unlikely to come up with "novel" ideas, but I restrained myself. Besides, I had gotten married out of the deal.

Four years later, I find myself appalled that nobody in the U.S. media includes the fact of our involvement in the Ethiopian invasion when writing about the current famine in Somalia. Increasingly, evidence shows that famines occur because of poor governance, not inadequate food, so our role in the country's destabilization deserves a mention.

There are now an estimated 1 million Somali refugees in Kenya, many of whom obtain refugee visas that allow them to enter the U.S. Are there Somali refugees in the U.S. who have a grudge against their adopted country? No doubt. The U.N. now estimates that 750,000 people may die as a result of the famine. Twenty-nine thousand children under the age of five have already died. This is a high price to pay for fighting al-Qaida, and Americans are not the ones paying it.

The two faces of America, one the benign visage of the Statue of Liberty, the other the aggrandizing militaristic empire, are hard to reconcile even if you grew up with them. Seeing my husband grapple with the enormous diversity of this country, the ethnicities, the politics, the class divisions and cultures, I can't imagine that Somalis are any less baffled, not to mention frustrated. And humiliated.

As the agent's questions wear on, my husband lapses into silence, letting me answer for him. I can see that the immigration guy is just doing his job, but the situation is terrifying and even though I can hear my braying, nervous laugh, I can't stop myself.

Satisfied with our answers, the agent tells us that he'll note that our marriage is "real," which will help us later. (Later?) There's just one thing: He is supposed to have a cop look through my husband's suitcase, but it's already been loaded onto the plane. He asks the airline people to hold the flight, promising them it will be only five minutes.

We follow the agent back to the jetway. Halfway down the corridor, he stops.

"Wait a minute," he says. "You should wait here so..."

"To save us embarrassment," I say.

"You got it." He smiles reassuringly. A minute later, he is back.

"They can't find it," he says. "But I'm afraid if they take it off now, it won't make it back on the plane with you. Just go ahead and get on the plane."

I look at him in amazement. Worried that the airline will lose our luggage, he is not going to bother to check it. We thank him and scurry onto the plane.

My husband is mortified. I feel badly for him, but I also feel the same way I have felt ever since I returned from Africa. I feel safe. I am relieved that my husband is here, and impatient for the day when we can bring his sons to live in a place where they can grow up without worrying about malaria or periodic political upheaval.

Unlike many of my left-wing friends, I take the threat of Islamic extremism seriously. I have heard the anti-American diatribes of imams blasting out of too many radios, lived in communities where Westerners have been kidnapped and killed by extremists, and witnessed the fear and anger instilled in my own stepsons by their madrassa. Certainly I worry that "the system" has the latitude to lock people away in places like Guantanamo Bay without a trial. But the immigration guy isn't responsible for American foreign policy. Inside the borders of our country, he was nice and respectful, which is more than you can say for government officials in Kenya. And in the end, we even made our flight.

Once we landed in San Francisco, I think we both felt a sense of relief, knowing the story was over. But there was a coda: My best friend, who is renting us her mother's apartment in San Francisco, told us that two FBI officers had showed up at her door the previous morning. Sensing that they weren't on high alert, she joked around, telling them I was more of a troublemaker than my husband, an easygoing guy whose only political activism was agitating for payment for his fellow players on a soccer team twenty years ago.

"I think they were just doing, what's the word, due diligence," she said.

I relay the story to my husband.

"The system works," I say. "What do you think?"

He points out that the security agents should have questioned him after he went through the TSA checkpoint, which would have saved him the embarrassment of being pulled off the plane.

"It could work better," he says.

Yeah, I think. And it could work a whole lot worse.

EIGHT

THE REFUGEE ALL-STARS

"I don't like war," said Reuben Koroma, leader of the Afro-pop band the Refugee All Stars. "I like pleasure."

While this sentiment may not be particularly novel for a musician, it takes on added meaning in Koroma's case. His musical group got together in a refugee camp in Guinea after fleeing a decade-long civil war in Sierra Leone. Not long ago, the band's six musicians had no reasonable expectation of making a CD, much less touring the U.S.

Their Cinderella story began when two American film-makers arrived in their refugee camp hoping to make a music documentary about the war that had transformed the small, diamond-rich West African country of Sierra Leone into the poster child for a failed state. The filmmakers, Zach Niles and Banker White (yes, that's his real name), found a group of musicians who were serious and professional, doggedly rehearsing as if their next gig was at the Kennedy Center instead of at a neighboring refugee camp. Under the circumstances, it was an act of faith that would have done Bob Marley, whom Koroma cites as his inspiration, proud.

The two filmmakers happened to come along when the

band got its first lucky break. When the United Nations told the refugees that it was safe to return to Sierra Leone, many were too frightened to leave the camps. Hoping to persuade them, the UN sponsored a 30-day trip to Free-town. For the Refugee All Stars, the chance to record a CD in a Freetown studio proved impossible to resist — at least for most of the band. One of the film's most touching moments comes when percussionist Mohammed, a haunted, sensitive-looking guy, comes down with a myste-rious flu-like illness on the day of departure. Anyone who has ever found it difficult to leave a safe place will recognize the look in his eyes.

For the rest of the band, the trip paid off handsomely. In a Freetown battle of the bands, the Refugee All Stars were named most promising new group. Last year, when the documentary on their journey began sweeping prizes on the film-festival circuit (six and counting), the producers found it easy to give the All Stars what every musician really wants: promotion. Since then, the Refugee All Stars have spent the summer touring the U.S., playing at Lincoln Center, the Kennedy Center and a host of other venues. Their managers are currently negotiating with a major label. The film's producers, Niles and White, originally greeted with the outdated pre-Bono attitude that "Africa doesn't sell" are also looking at a mainstream distribution deal.

The word used to describe the Refugee All Stars sound, a combination of reggae, traditional West African music, and hip-hop, is infectious. That's not a term most people associate with Sierra Leone, a country best known for the rebels, many of them child soldiers, who cut off the hands and feet of ordinary people in a gruesome campaign of intimidation in the 1990s.

The music is indeed infectious, but what's more important is that the Refugee All Stars offer an alternate view of
Africa, a glimpse into a joyful and life-affirming spirit that
we can only hope, in this era of onrushing globalization, is
hard-wired into all of us.

ACKNOWLEDGMENTS

Earlier versions of several of these essays were published in the *LA Weekly*, *Truthdig*, and the *Tucson Weekly*. I am grateful to my editors, Joe Donnelly, James Reel, and Peter Scheer. I remain deeply indebted to the International Center for Journalists in Washington, D.C., and to the Sen. John Heinz Fellowship in Environmental Reporting. Sending me to Madagascar changed the course of my career and gave me much-needed perspective on America's current dilemmas.

Special shoutout to Peter Scheer for the best headlines in the business.

www.ingramcontent.com/pod-product-compliance
Lightning Source LLC
Chambersburg PA
CBHW021430110726
47901CB00008B/2374